WHERE TO GO AND WHAT TO DO ON LONG ISLAND

by SCOPE
(Suffolk County Organization for the
Promotion of Education)

DOVER PUBLICATIONS, INC.
New York

Note: East Norwich, Muttontown Preserve, Kings Point and the American Merchant Marine Museum, and the United States Merchant Marine Academy are actually located in Nassau County (and not Suffolk County as is indicated at various points in the text).

Published in Canada by General Publishing Company, Ltd., 30 Lesmill Road, Don Mills, Toronto, Ontario.

Published in the United Kingdom by Constable and Company, Ltd., 3 The Lanchesters, 162–164 Fulham Palace Road, London W6 9ER.

Where to Go and What to Do on Long Island is a new work, first published by Dover Publications, Inc., in 1993. Fred Monner—consultant.

Manufactured in the United States of America
Dover Publications, Inc., 31 East 2nd Street, Mineola, N.Y. 11501

Library of Congress Cataloging-in-Publication Data

Where to go and what to do on Long Island / SCOPE, Suffolk County Organization for the Promotion of Education.
    p.   cm.
  ISBN 0-486-27162-5
  1. Long Island (N.Y.)—Guidebooks. 2. New York Region—Guidebooks. I. Suffolk County Organization for the Promotion of Education (Suffolk County, N.Y.)
F127.L8W54   1993
917.47′210443—dc20
                                                              92-37112
                                                                 CIP

CONTENTS

SUFFOLK COUNTY

ADDENDA

MAP REFERENCE

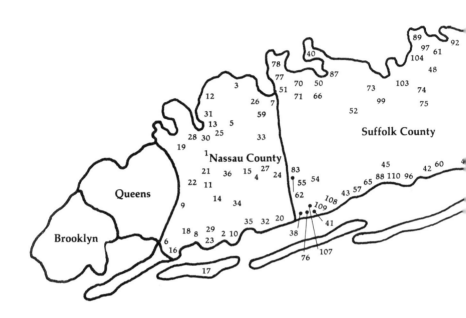

NASSAU COUNTY

1. Albertson
2. Baldwin
3. Bayville
4. Bethpage
5. Brookville
6. Cedarhurst
7. Cold Spring Harbor
8. East Rockaway
9. Elmont
10. Freeport
11. Garden City
12. Glen Cove
13. Greenvale
14. Hempstead
15. Hicksville
16. Lawrence
17. Long Beach
18. Lynbrook
19. Manhasset
20. Massapequa
21. Mineola
22. New Hyde Park
23. Oceanside
24. Old Bethpage
25. Old Westbury
26. Oyster Bay
27. Plainview
28. Port Washington
29. Rockville Centre
30. Roslyn
31. Sea Cliff
32. Seaford
33. Syosset
34. Uniondale
35. Wantagh
36. Westbury

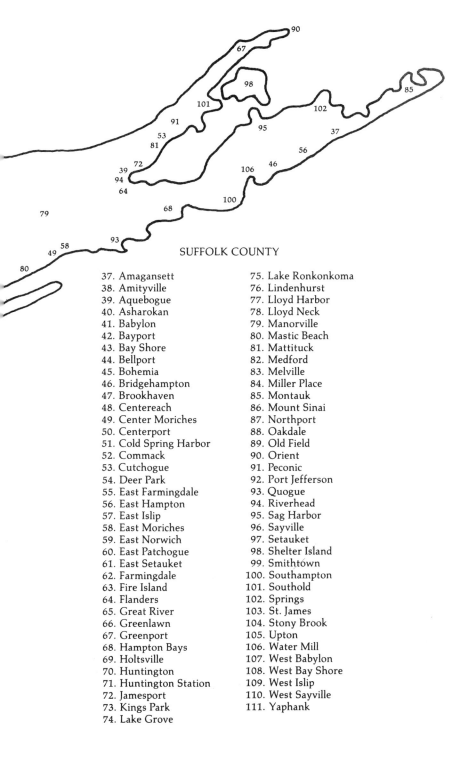

SUFFOLK COUNTY

37. Amagansett
38. Amityville
39. Aquebogue
40. Asharokan
41. Babylon
42. Bayport
43. Bay Shore
44. Bellport
45. Bohemia
46. Bridgehampton
47. Brookhaven
48. Centereach
49. Center Moriches
50. Centerport
51. Cold Spring Harbor
52. Commack
53. Cutchogue
54. Deer Park
55. East Farmingdale
56. East Hampton
57. East Islip
58. East Moriches
59. East Norwich
60. East Patchogue
61. East Setauket
62. Farmingdale
63. Fire Island
64. Flanders
65. Great River
66. Greenlawn
67. Greenport
68. Hampton Bays
69. Holtsville
70. Huntington
71. Huntington Station
72. Jamesport
73. Kings Park
74. Lake Grove

75. Lake Ronkonkoma
76. Lindenhurst
77. Lloyd Harbor
78. Lloyd Neck
79. Manorville
80. Mastic Beach
81. Mattituck
82. Medford
83. Melville
84. Miller Place
85. Montauk
86. Mount Sinai
87. Northport
88. Oakdale
89. Old Field
90. Orient
91. Peconic
92. Port Jefferson
93. Quogue
94. Riverhead
95. Sag Harbor
96. Sayville
97. Setauket
98. Shelter Island
99. Smithtown
100. Southampton
101. Southold
102. Springs
103. St. James
104. Stony Brook
105. Upton
106. Water Mill
107. West Babylon
108. West Bay Shore
109. West Islip
110. West Sayville
111. Yaphank

INTRODUCTION

EVEN IF YOU HAVE LIVED a lifetime on Long Island exploring its highways and back roads, you will find this a book of revelation—of places you never knew existed and things you never knew before.

For the casual visitor or vacationer, city dwellers looking for a change of pace, teachers and group leaders planning field trips, sportsmen, students, nature lovers, history buffs, sun worshippers, families, adventurous senior citizens and singles—in fact, for anyone looking for fun, excitement or pleasurable learning— these pages open the door to a treasure trove of places to go and things to do. Here you will find information on visiting parks, museums, historic buildings, recreational facilities, communications centers, businesses, industries, nature and science centers and government and public service institutions.

Make your Sunday outing or your vacation trip more meaningful by planning to stop off at one or several of the many places of interest to be found along your route. Keep this book handy as a reference to the sights of Long Island and its culture, history, resources and natural beauty. Take young people out into the world that surrounds Long Island schools with invaluable educational experiences. The information on each site includes a recommendation as to appropriateness for various grade levels, facilities available and charges, if any. Teachers will discover many possibilities: going to hospitals for health education, to Walt Whitman's birthplace in connection with poetry or to Home Sweet Home in connection with music.

All information about places of interest contained in this book has been carefully checked and updated. If changes occur, for instance in telephone numbers, revised information can be obtained from telephone directories, Chambers of Commerce or local governments. All telephone numbers are (516) area code, except where otherwise indicated. Also, note that the word "to" as in "June to September" should be understood as meaning "to and including." The book is divided into two sections, Nassau County and Suffolk County, and is alphabetized first by municipality, then by institution within a given municipality.

NASSAU COUNTY

Clark Botanic Garden of the Town of North Hempstead

CLARK BOTANIC GARDEN occupies 12 rolling acres in Albertson, adjacent to the Albertson LIRR Station, in central Nassau County. The aim of the Garden is to convey the beauty, fascination and importance of the plant world. Horticultural and landscape features include three ponds, a canopy of mature white pines and hemlocks, extensive woody plantings, a rose garden, an herb garden, a daylily garden, a wildflower garden, an iris garden, an early-flowering garden, a rock garden, a dwarf conifer garden, perennials and annuals. Programs are for adults and children, registered individually or in groups. Subject areas include gardening, botany, nature and the environment. Clark Botanic Garden is a living catalog of landscape ideas for the home gardener.

Address/Telephone	193 I.U. Willets Road
	Albertson, NY 11507
	484-8600
When to Visit	Monday to Sunday
	10:30 a.m. to 4:30 p.m.
	Call for possible holiday closings
	Groups by appointment
Charges/Fees	Residents of North Hempstead free admission
	Non-resident adults—$4.00
	Non-resident children and senior citizens—$3.00
Suggested Grades	4–Adult
Guided Tour	Yes, by special arrangement

Maximum Group	60
Group Notice	2 weeks
Eating Facilities	Picnic area
Restroom Facilities	Yes
Handicapped Access	No
Additional Information	Special programs are offered for children in grades 4–6 and for adults. Off-site programs are available in North Hempstead. Special events include plant sales, music concerts, a Halloween Spooky Walk, Earth Day celebration, a late-summer Seniors Day and a Fall Festival. Clark Botanic Garden is a Division of the Town of North Hempstead Parks & Recreation Department.

Baldwin Historical Museum

HOUSED IN ITS headquarters built for the bicentennial, the Baldwin Historical Society's young but growing museum contains photographs, artifacts and memorabilia from Baldwin's past.

Address/Telephone	1980 Grand Avenue Baldwin, NY 11510 223-6900
When to Visit	Monday, Wednesday and Friday 9:00 a.m. to 11:30 a.m. Sunday—1:00 p.m. to 4:00 p.m. Groups by appointment
Charges/Fees	None
Suggested Grades	3–Adult
Guided Tour	Yes, 30 minutes, by appointment.
Maximum Group	30
Group Notice	3 weeks
Eating Facilities	None

Restroom Facilities	Yes
Handicapped Access	No
Additional Information	Slide presentations available. Single floor access for handicapped.

Bayville Historical Museum

THE DEVELOPMENT OF the Village of Bayville is displayed in several interpretive permanent exhibitions including a room dedicated to the late billionaire Harrison Williams and his wife, Mona, whose opulent estate in Bayville was known as "Oak Point." Two murals depict the magnificent oriental gardens which once flourished on the estate. Another mural enhances the shellfish industry exhibit. Farm equipment, and the history of the once-thriving asparagus industry in the Village, are on permanent display. Other permanent exhibits include a turn-of-the-century classroom; antique home furnishings, ca. 1850–1930; a hands-on costume closet and a country store. The Museum's main attractions are seasonal rotating exhibitions and "Create-a-Creature" workshops where visitors decorate the "rubber plush" designs of T. Oliver Kopian.

Address/Telephone	34 School Street Bayville, NY 11709 628-2011 or 628-1720
When to Visit	Wednesday and Sunday. Holidays and summer months by appointment. Noon to 4:00 p.m. School and other groups by appointment
Charges/Fees	Free; however, there is a charge for "Creature" materials.
Suggested Grades	2–Adult (Varies with program)
Guided Tour	Yes, from 30 minutes to 1 hour or more depending on participation.
Maximum Group	30
Group Notice	2 weeks minimum
Eating Facilities	None
Restroom Facilities	Yes

Handicapped Access	To most exhibition areas
Additional Information	It is best to call Lorraine Cocomero, Director/ Curator at 628-2011 or 628-1720 for updated information.

Zorn's Poultry Farm

THIS RETAIL FACILITY contains a small outdoor farm and zoo where youngsters may see and feed turkeys, rabbits and several varieties of chickens, including some rare exotic types. Ready-to-cook and ready-to-eat poultry may be purchased here.

Address/Telephone	4321 Hempstead Turnpike Bethpage, NY 11714–5798 731-5500
When to Visit	Daily 9:00 a.m. to 8:00 p.m. Avoid weeks before Thanksgiving and Christmas
Charges/Fees	None
Suggested Grades	Pre-K–4
Guided Tour	None
Maximum Group	40, with 1 adult per group of 10
Group Notice	None
Eating Facilities	None
Restroom Facilities	None
Handicapped Access	No
Additional Information	Extra safety precautions are needed in parking lot.

Tilles Center for the Performing Arts
(Long Island University/C.W. Post Campus)

THERE ARE FEW halls in the nation with the acoustics, sightlines and performing space to match the excellence of this concert theater. Concerts, lectures and other cultural events take place throughout the year.

Address/Telephone	Northern Boulevard Brookville, NY 11548 626-3100
When to Visit	Write or call for most recent schedule
Charges/Fees	Varies with program
Suggested Grades	K–Adult, depending on program
Guided Tour	None
Maximum Group	Unlimited
Group Notice	Depends on program
Eating Facilities	Yes, by arrangement
Restroom Facilities	Yes
Handicapped Access	Yes
Additional Information	Subscriptions available, contact box office. Infrared hearing assistance system.

Loring Art Gallery

THIS GALLERY EXHIBITS the work of major contemporary American artists. There is a fine collection of contemporary graphics and an impressive group of 19th-century French posters. Exhibits are constantly changing and all works on display are for sale.

Address/Telephone	661 Central Avenue Cedarhurst, NY 11516 295-1919
When to Visit	10:30 a.m. to 5:00 p.m. Closed Tuesday and Sunday
Charges/Fees	None
Suggested Grades	9–Adult
Guided Tour	None
Maximum Group	20
Group Notice	1 month
Eating Facilities	None
Restroom Facilities	Yes
Handicapped Access	No

Cold Spring Harbor Fish Hatchery and Aquarium

THIS HATCHERY WAS established in 1883 by New York State. Visitors will see New York State's largest collection of native freshwater fish, reptiles and amphibians, housed in 40 aquariums, indoor and outdoor turtle habitats, a 20-foot indoor stream exhibit and an amphibian display. Fish in the six outdoor ponds may be seen in various stages of their growth cycle. There are three buildings on the site: The Main Aquarium Building, the Fairchild Exhibit Building and the Hatch House. The hatchery is located on the south side of Route 25A, just west of the Nassau–Suffolk border.

Address/Telephone	*Route 25A (west of Nassau–Suffolk border) Cold Spring Harbor, NY 11724 692-6768
When to Visit	Daily 10:00 a.m. to 5:00 p.m. Closed Christmas and Thanksgiving

Charges/Fees	Adults—$2.50; children (5–12) and seniors—$1.25;
	  children under 5 and members—free
	Programs: $2.00 per person/1-hour program;
	  $4.00 per person/2-hour program

Suggested Grades	All ages
Guided Tour	Organized groups and schools call for arrangements
Maximum Group	20–25, with a maximum of three groups at one time depending upon program
Group Notice	Call for reservation as soon as possible
Eating Facilities	None
Restroom Facilities	Yes
Handicapped Access	Yes
Additional Information	Visitors may feed the fish. Call for information on special programs. *Mailing address: P.O. Box 535, Cold Spring Harbor, NY 11724

Old Grist Mill Museum

L OCATED IN THE oldest building in Nassau County, this one-time grist mill is now home to a museum. There are many types of exhibitions in addition to the milling area, including a barber shop, dental office, a store and blacksmith shop. A scale model of East Rockaway, c. 1900, is also on display. The museum is recovering from a disastrous fire that occurred in 1990, but still welcomes visitors.

Address/Telephone	Woods and Atlantic Avenues East Rockaway, NY 11518 599-4999
When to Visit	Saturday and Sunday Memorial Day to Labor Day 1:00 p.m. to 5:00 p.m. Groups by appointment
Charges/Fees	None
Suggested Grades	K–Adult
Guided Tour	None
Maximum Group	Unlimited
Group Notice	None
Eating Facilities	None
Restroom Facilities	None
Handicapped Access	No

Breakfast at Belmont

W HILE EATING BREAKFAST in the trackside café, you can relax and watch the horses breeze through their morning workouts on the racing oval. NYRA commentators are on hand to share Belmont history and present interviews with jockeys, trainers and other racing personalities. When visiting the Paddock, track personnel will demonstrate the techniques and equipment used in grooming, training and riding. A tour of the Backstretch will give visitors a view of the starting gate and barn area.

Address/Telephone	*Belmont Racetrack Hempstead Avenue Elmont, NY 11003 (718) 641-4700, ext. 4494
When to Visit	Daily except Tuesdays Approximately: May 10 to July 30 and August 29 to October 22 7:30 a.m. to 10:00 a.m. Call for exact dates and events
Charges/Fees	Parking and admission Breakfast at reasonable prices
Suggested Grades	K–Adult
Guided Tour	Yes, 30 minutes
Maximum Group	60, with adequate supervision
Group Notice	1 week
Eating Facilities	Yes
Restroom Facilities	Yes
Handicapped Access	Yes
Additional Information	*Mailing address: Customer Service Dept., N.Y. Racing Association, P.O. Box 90, Jamaica, NY 11417

Collector's Cars Museum

THIS MUSEUM/WORKSHOP displays up to 30 and more restored antique automobiles. Some of the world's finest exotic and vintage automobiles may be found at Collector's Cars, Inc. A fully equipped restoration shop is located right on the premises. Visitors may observe all aspects of auto restoration including structural rebuilding, panel fabrication, leadwork, painting and interior reconstruction. For the antique auto enthusiast, lease or purchase arrangements can be made during or after visits.

Address/Telephone	56 W. Merrick Road Freeport, NY 11520 378-6666

When to Visit	Monday, Tuesday, Wednesday and Saturday 9:00 a.m. to 6:00 p.m.
Charges/Fees	None
Suggested Grades	4–Adult
Guided Tour	None
Maximum Group	20, with adequate supervision
Group Notice	1 week
Eating Facilities	None
Restroom Facilities	Yes
Handicapped Access	No
Additional Information	Enter though front door. Special welcome to senior citizens.

Freeport Historical Society Museum

THIS MUSEUM SPECIALIZES in local heritage. Emphasis is placed on the evolution of the local histories of Freeport and the surrounding villages, the vaudeville era and shipwrecks along the nearby coast.

Address/Telephone	350 South Main Street Freeport, NY 11520 623-9632
When to Visit	May to December
Charges/Fees	Donation
Suggested Grades	3–Adult
Guided Tour	Yes, 1 hour for schools and groups by appointment
Maximum Group	25
Group Notice	3 weeks
Eating Facilities	None
Restroom Facilities	Yes
Handicapped Access	No
Additional Information	During winter months "Museum in the Box" program is available to Freeport schools.

Firehouse Gallery
(Nassau Community College)

VISITORS WILL SEE art exhibits featuring painting, sculpture, crafts, prints, drawings and photography. These change monthly. There are also lectures, demonstrations and speakers each month. The gallery also sponsors competitions in the various art mediums.

Address/Telephone	Nassau Community College Garden City, NY 11530 222-7165
When to Visit	Monday to Thursday—11:30 a.m. to 4:30 p.m. Tuesday to Thursday—7:00 p.m. to 10:00 p.m. Saturday and Sunday—1:00 p.m. to 5:00 p.m.
Charges/Fees	None
Suggested Grades	3–Adult
Guided Tour	Yes, by appointment, 30 minutes
Maximum Group	50, with 1 adult per group of 25
Group Notice	Call in advance
Eating Facilities	Yes, nearby
Restroom Facilities	Yes
Handicapped Access	Yes

Long Island Lighting Company
(LILCO)

LILCO IS PLEASED to invite school and community groups to tour its facilities. Visitors will learn about electricity and gas from the people that provide these vital services to the residents and businesses of Long Island. Tours include visits to LILCO's electric and gas control centers and computer centers in Hicksville and the training facility in Central Islip.

Address/Telephone	550 Stewart Avenue Garden City, NY 11530 933-5292 Call: Community Relations Dept.

When to Visit	By appointment
Charges/Fees	None
Suggested Grades	3–Adult
Guided Tour	Yes, 1 hour
Maximum Group	20
Group Notice	Call for appointment
Eating Facilities	None
Restroom Facilities	Yes
Handicapped Access	Yes
Additional Information	Call for specific arrangements suited to your group's age or needs. Teaching kits are also available for Natural Gas Safety Programs.

Garvies Point Museum and Preserve

THE CENTERPIECE OF a 62-acre preserve overlooking Long Island Sound, the museum specializes in the archaeology and geology of the area. Five miles of nature trails offer a diversified look at the natural surroundings and habitat of the north shore of Long Island. Changing exhibits from seashells to minerals to dugout canoes inform and educate visitors about the natural heritage of the land.

Address/Telephone	Barry Drive Glen Cove, NY 11542 671-0300
When to Visit	Preserve: 8:30 a.m. to dusk Closed Mondays Museum hours: Tuesday to Saturday 10:00 a.m. to 4:00 p.m. Sunday—1:00 p.m. to 4:00 p.m. Groups by appointment Tuesday to Friday
Charges/Fees	Adults—$1.00 Children—$.50 Educational program—$25.00 (plus $.50 per student)
Suggested Grades	K–Adult

Guided Tour	Museum education program groups by appointment
Maximum Group	30, with 1 adult per group of 10
Group Notice	3 weeks
Eating Facilities	Picnic facilities nearby
Restroom Facilities	Yes
Handicapped Access	Yes
Additional Information	No collecting, digging or cliff climbing. Educational programs rain or shine; dress appropriately. Operated by the Nassau County Department of Recreation and Parks.

Welwyn Preserve

THIS 200-ACRE nature preserve bordering on Long Island Sound has on its grounds a field ecology study station that provides prime examples of a mixed deciduous forest, a stream valley, a freshwater pond, a salt marsh and a beach.

Address/Telephone	Crescent Beach Road Glen Cove, NY 11542 Education Center: 676-1483
When to Visit	Wednesday to Sunday (excluding holidays) June 1 to October 15 9:30 a.m. to 4:30 p.m.
Charges/Fees	Visit free. Fee for educational programs—$20.00.
Suggested Grades	1–Adult, depending on program and group size
Guided Tour	Yes, length and scope depending on needs
Maximum Group	Varies with program
Group Notice	1 month
Eating Facilities	"Brown bag"
Restroom Facilities	Yes
Handicapped Access	No

Additional Information Reservations for educational programs should be made well in advance of the visit. Operated by the Nassau County Department of Recreation and Parks.

Eglevsky Ballet of New York

THE EGLEVSKY BALLET COMPANY is perhaps best known for its annual presentation of *The Nutcracker*. In addition to that magical ballet, this company presents beloved works of the classical ballet tradition and also serves as a showcase for the work of some of America's most promising contemporary choreographers.

Address/Telephone *Tilles Center
C. W. Post Campus
Northern Boulevard
Greenvale, NY 11548
746-1115
and
Hofstra University
John Cranford Adam Playhouse
Hempstead, NY 11550

When to Visit Call or write for schedule

Charges/Fees Varies with program

Suggested Grades K–Adult, depending on program

Guided Tour None

Maximum Group 500

Group Notice 2 to 4 weeks for groups

Eating Facilities None

Restroom Facilities Yes

Handicapped Access Yes

Additional Information *Mailing address: 999 Herricks Road at Shelter Rock Road, New Hyde Park, NY 11040

Hillwood Art Museum
(C. W. Post Campus)

HILLWOOD ART MUSEUM is part of Long Island University's C. W. Post Campus. The museum is located in the Hillwood Commons building that also has a restaurant and cafeteria. Recipient of national and state funding. The exhibits, catalogs, lecture series and programs have brought Hillwood Art Gallery a positive response from artists, critics and curators. Exhibits change about every eight weeks.

Address/Telephone	Northern Boulevard Greenvale, NY 11548 299-2788
When to Visit	Monday to Friday—10:00 a.m. to 5:00 p.m. Sunday—1:00 p.m. to 5:00 p.m.
Charges/Fees	None
Suggested Grades	4–Adult
Guided Tour	None
Maximum Group	25, with adequate supervision
Group Notice	None
Eating Facilities	Yes, cafeteria
Restroom Facilities	Yes
Handicapped Access	Yes

Long Island Philharmonic Society

THE LONG ISLAND PHILHARMONIC is composed of 95 highly regarded, full-time professional musicians. The group has now become one of the finest ensembles in the nation. In its superb new home at Tilles Center, as well as other halls, the Long Island Philharmonic has become the crown jewel of Long Island's cultural life. Aside from entertaining the region's adult community, it also performs young persons' concerts for large audiences of children.

Long Island Philharmonic

Address/Telephone	*Tilles Center C. W. Post Campus Northern Boulevard Greenvale, NY 11548 293-2222, 293-2223
When to Visit	Call or write for schedule
Charges/Fees	Varies with program
Suggested Grades	K–Adult, depending on program
Guided Tour	None
Maximum Group	500–2,000 depending on location
Group Notice	2 weeks
Eating Facilities	None
Restroom Facilities	Yes
Handicapped Access	Yes
Additional Information	Braille program notes available. Master class programs available. *Mailing address: One Huntington Quadrangle, Suite LL09, Melville, NY 11747

Fine Arts Museum of Long Island

FAMLI HAS A growing permanent collection of contemporary and primitive art, featuring continuous professionally planned exhibits. In addition, the museum offers special programs such as lectures, symposiums, slide demonstrations, exhibit-related workshops, a computer imaging center, a photographic center and a pre-Columbian section. We also have a Computer Imaging Center to display the work of computer-assisted art, with 4 computers set up so that visitors can work with computer graphics.

Address/Telephone	295 Fulton Avenue Hempstead, NY 11550 481-5700
When to Visit	Wednesday to Saturday 10:00 a.m. to 4:00 p.m. Groups: Call Coordinator of Educational Services for appointments
Charges/Fees	By arrangement
Suggested Grades	K–Adult
Guided Tour	Yes, 60 to 90 minutes by arrangement
Maximum Group	By arrangement
Group Notice	1 month
Eating Facilities	None
Restroom Facilities	Yes
Handicapped Access	One level for handicapped
Additional Information	Special programs for handicapped and grade school children available.

Hofstra Museum
(Hofstra University)

THE MUSEUM IS comprised of Emily Lowe Gallery, Filderman Gallery, Lowenfeld Exhibition hall, Calkins Gallery and a sculpture garden with over 45 works. Visitors will observe numerous exhibitions of a wide variety of paintings, sculpture, prints and photography on display throughout the year. Included are European paintings from the 16th–20th centuries and marble sculptures of the 19th century, as well as an outstanding collection of 20th-century American art. There is an impressive collection of tribal art and an important collection of Oriental sculpture and paintings, Oceanic, pre-Columbian and African art.

Address/Telephone	Hofstra University Hempstead Turnpike Hempstead, NY 11550 463-5672
When to Visit	Tuesday—10:00 a.m. to 9:00 p.m. Wednesday to Friday—10:00 a.m. to 5:00 p.m. Saturday and Sunday—1:00 p.m. to 5:00 p.m. Closed Mondays and holidays
Charges/Fees	None
Suggested Grades	1–Adult
Guided Tour	Yes, 40 minutes
Maximum Group	20, with 1 adult per group of 10
Group Notice	2 weeks
Eating Facilities	Yes, campus cafeteria
Restroom Facilities	Yes
Handicapped Access	Yes

Nassau–Suffolk Braille Library

OPERATED BY THE Helen Keller Services for the Blind, this is actually more a publishing house, bindery and distribution center. It produces and circulates nearly 25,000 braille and large-type textbooks to hundreds of blind students, thus enabling them to attend a regular school near home. Visitors will see employees and volunteers transcribing, copying, collating, binding and packing the volumes.

Address/Telephone	320 Fulton Avenue Hempstead, NY 11550 485-1234 Call: Mrs. Edith Magee

When to Visit	Monday to Friday 9:00 a.m. to 4:30 p.m.
Charges/Fees	None
Suggested Grades	7–Adult
Guided Tour	Yes, 1 hour
Maximum Group	30
Group Notice	2 weeks
Eating Facilities	None
Restroom Facilities	Yes
Handicapped Access	No

The Hicksville Gregory Museum
(Long Island Earth Science Center)

THE HICKSVILLE GREGORY MUSEUM, with the largest mineral collection on Long Island, features over 4,000 specimens of rocks and minerals, including fluorescent displays. Located in the original Heitz Place Court House, a national historic site, the museum also displays changing historic exhibits. The Old Court House Jail, one of the few "Old Town Lock-ups" still surviving, is open to the inspection of curious visitors.

Address/Telephone	Heitz Place & Bay Avenue Hicksville, NY 11801 822-7505
When to Visit	Monday by appointment Tuesday to Friday—9:30 a.m. to 4:30 p.m. Saturday and Sunday—1:00 p.m. to 5:00 p.m.
Charges/Fees	Adults—$2.50; senior citizens—$1.25; children 5 to 17—$1.25 Schools and groups: Students (tour included)—$2.50 Children under 5, members and Hicksville residents free
Suggested Grades	K–Adult
Guided Tour	Yes, 1 to 2 hours

Maximum Group	50, with 1 adult per group of 10
Group Notice	1 month minimum
Eating Facilities	None
Restroom Facilities	Yes
Handicapped Access	Yes
Additional Information	Slide and lecture programs available.

Rock Hall Museum

RISING MAJESTICALLY FROM the modern landscape along Broadway in the Village of Lawrence, Rock Hall captures the spirit and history of our town's colonial era. Visitors marvel at the exquisitely preserved Georgian architecture and decoration of this over 200-year-old house. The magnificent white mansion contains period dining, game and drawing rooms, a complete kitchen and authentic bedrooms. Each room is a vivid example of how early town settlers lived and played. Picnic tables in the museum's colorful garden, offer a serene setting for lunch or afternoon rest. The area also serves as a gathering point for scheduled outdoor events. In addition to an educational program for students, the museum offers a variety of exhibits. A seasonal closing begins November 30 with a reopening set for April 1.

Address/Telephone	199 Broadway
	Lawrence, NY 11559
	239-1157
When to Visit	April to November
	Weekdays (Closed Tuesday)—10:00 a.m. to 4:00 p.m.
	Sunday—Noon to 4:00 p.m.
Charges/Fees	None
Suggested Grades	K–Adult
Guided Tour	Yes, 45 minutes
Maximum Group	30, with 1 adult per group of 10
Group Notice	Call for appointment
Eating Facilities	Yes, picnic facilities
Restroom Facilities	Yes
Handicapped Access	No

Long Beach Memorial Hospital

L ONG BEACH MEMORIAL Hospital and Nursing Home is a 403-bed
medical center, teaching hospital and skilled nursing home. State of
the art diagnostic, medical and surgical procedures performed here are
comparable to large hospitals. Virtually every medical service except
obstetrics and every surgical procedure except open heart surgery and
organ transplants are performed at this facility.

Address/Telephone	455 E. Bay Drive
	Long Beach, NY 11561
	432-8000, ext. 2362—Community Relations
When to Visit	By appointment
Charges/Fees	None
Suggested Grades	K–Adult
Guided Tour	Yes, 1 hour
Maximum Group	25
Group Notice	2 weeks
Eating Facilities	None
Restroom Facilities	Yes
Handicapped Access	Yes
Additional Information	Call in advance with information relative to group ages, focus of interest, etc.

Fantasy Playhouse
(Theatre Workshop)

F ANTASY PLAYHOUSE PRODUCES Broadway revivals using professional
actors, and original musicals based on children's classics featuring
students of the Playhouse's theater school. The Playhouse is open all year
with classes for children, teens and adults and performances geared to all
age groups. It also brings shows to schools, camps and libraries.

Address/Telephone	317 Merrick Road
	Lynbrook, NY 11563
	599-1982

When to Visit	Call or write for schedule
Charges/Fees	Call or write for information
Suggested Grades	K–Adult
Guided Tour	None
Maximum Group	135
Group Notice	2 weeks
Eating Facilities	None
Restroom Facilities	Yes
Handicapped Access	No
Additional Information	Theater programs presented at your school—musical/drama/comedy—by arrangement.

The Science Museum of Long Island

THE SCIENCE MUSEUM of Long Island is a science education activity center. It was formed to stimulate children's interest in science and provide them with opportunities to participate in the excitement of discovery, to involve the adult public in the world of science and to expand the community's interest in our natural environment.

Address/Telephone	1526 N. Plandome Road Manhasset, NY 11030 627-9400
When to Visit	Monday to Friday—9:00 a.m. to 5:00 p.m. Saturday and Sunday—11:00 a.m. to 4:00 p.m. Program requests by appointment only
Charges/Fees	By arrangement
Suggested Grades	Pre-K–Adult
Guided Tour	Yes, 60 to 90 minutes
Maximum Group	100
Group Notice	1 week
Eating Facilities	Indoor and outdoor picnic facilities
Restroom Facilities	Yes
Handicapped Access	No

John F. Kennedy Wildlife Sanctuary

THIS AQUATIC-ORIENTED outdoor wildlife area is located on over 500 acres of tidal marshlands. One can hike along an old road to any of several blinds or to the observation tower from which one may train one's glasses toward the pond and treetops to view numerous varieties of birds and wildlife.

Address/Telephone	*Tobay Beach Massapequa, NY 11758 795-1000
When to Visit	Memorial Day to Labor Day—4:30 p.m. to dark Winter—8:00 a.m. to dark Permit required (no charge)—Applications available at address below
Charges/Fees	None
Suggested Grades	3–Adult
Guided Tour	None
Maximum Group	Unlimited
Group Notice	1 month
Eating Facilities	None
Restroom Facilities	Yes, nearby
Handicapped Access	No
Additional Information	*Mailing address: c/o Town of Oyster Bay, Dept. of Parks, 977 Hicksville Rd., Massapequa, NY 11758

Old Grace Church Museum
(Historical Society of the Massapequas)

OLD GRACE CHURCH, the oldest church in Massapequa, was erected by members of the Floyd-Jones family in 1844. The church, with its stained glass windows, offers an excellent example of church architecture of the period. A c. 1880 house located on the church grounds offers an excellent example of a working-class house of the period.

Address/Telephone	*Cedar Shore Drive and Merrick Road Massapequa, NY 11758 799-4676
When to Visit	Sunday 2:30 p.m. to 4:30 p.m. Open to public and groups by appointment
Charges/Fees	None
Suggested Grades	4–Adult
Guided Tour	Yes, 1 hour
Maximum Group	50
Group Notice	1 month
Eating Facilities	None
Restroom Facilities	Yes
Handicapped Access	No
Additional Information	Parking lot. Historic Floyd-Jones Cemetery in rear. *Mailing address: 106 Toronto Ave., Massapequa, NY 11758

Nassau County Board of Supervisors

THE NASSAU BOARD of Supervisors is the legislative branch of the County government. Its six members are the top elected officials of the County's major units, represented by the Presiding Supervisor and Supervisors of Hempstead, North Hempstead and Oyster Bay Townships, the City of Long Beach and the Mayor-Supervisor of the City of Glen Cove. The Board is empowered by the Nassau County Charter to enact local laws and adopt the County budget.

Address/Telephone	Nassau County Executive Building One West Street Mineola, NY 11501 535-4253
When to Visit	By appointment
Charges/Fees	None
Suggested Grades	9–Adult

Guided Tour	Yes, 20-minute orientation
Maximum Group	By arrangement
Group Notice	2 weeks
Eating Facilities	Yes
Restroom Facilities	Yes
Handicapped Access	Yes
Additional Information	The Board of Supervisors meets on Mondays. Check each month for calendar of meetings and hearings.

Nassau County Courts

THIS TRIP OFFERS students a special lecture on the criminal justice system and court systems of New York State and Nassau County. If the court calendar permits, an opportunity will be afforded to witness an actual courtroom trial. Other courtroom proceedings such as jury selection, cross examination, verdicts and sentencing may possibly be observed.

Address/Telephone	100 Supreme Court Drive Mineola, NY 11501 535-2013
When to Visit	Tuesday to Thursday 9:30 a.m. to 12:30 p.m.
Charges/Fees	None
Suggested Grades	11–Adult
Guided Tour	Yes, 3 hours for orientation and observation
Maximum Group	40
Group Notice	Make arrangements as early as possible
Eating Facilities	Yes, cafeteria
Restroom Facilities	Yes
Handicapped Access	Yes

Additional Information Speakers available to schools. Call: above and Nassau County Bar Association (747-4070).

To attend special demonstration trials write to: Michael F. Rich, Jr., Court Information Office, N.Y. State Supreme Court, Mineola, NY 11501

Nassau County Police Department

DEPENDING ON THE age and interests of the visitor, this visit can include a film on police operations and a walk through the 911 Emergency Communications Center, police museum and detention cell area. Other tours include the Mounted Unit and Children's Safety Town.

Address/Telephone	1490 Franklin Avenue Mineola, NY 11501 573-7135
When to Visit	Monday to Friday 10:00 a.m. to 1:00 p.m.
Charges/Fees	None
Suggested Grades	3–Adult
Guided Tour	Yes, 1 hour
Maximum Group	25, with adequate supervision
Group Notice	2 weeks
Eating Facilities	None
Restroom Facilities	Yes
Handicapped Access	Yes
Additional Information	Special classroom programs available. For tours of local police precincts in Nassau County, contact the commanding officer of the individual precinct.

Nassau County Police Museum

Nassau County Police Museum

THIS MUSEUM SERVES as a repository of artifacts collected during the 67 years of the Nassau County Police Department's service to the public. Exhibits include a 1925 Harley Davidson motorcycle with sidecar and a stationhouse scene from the early days. Also on display are confiscated weapons, laboratory equipment, badges, air and marine gear and many photographs depicting Department activity since 1925.

Address/Telephone   Police Headquarters
1490 Franklin Avenue
Mineola, NY 11501
573-7000

When to Visit	Monday to Friday 9:00 a.m. to 3:00 p.m. By special appointment—Call prior to visiting museum
Charges/Fees	None
Suggested Grades	K–Adult
Guided Tour	By appointment: 573-7620—Individuals 573-7135—Groups
Maximum Group	35
Group Notice	1 month
Eating Facilities	None
Restroom Facilities	Yes
Handicapped Access	Yes

Goudreau Museum of Mathematics in Art and Science (The Math Museum)

THIS ONE-ROOM museum and ancillary classroom space is bursting with puzzles, colorful geometric sculptures and math games. The "Math Museum's" message is that math is fun. A variety of activities and programs proves that message to be true. The facility is basically a workshop-type museum that features hands-on learning experiences.

Address/Telephone	Herrick Community Center 999 Herricks Road (Rm. 202) New Hyde Park, NY 11040-1302 747-0777
When to Visit	Monday to Saturday General public and groups by appointment only First Saturday of each month—open house October to May—Noon to 2:00 p.m.
Charges/Fees	Call for most recent fee schedule
Suggested Grades	K–Adult

Guided Tour	Variety of programs (most 2 hours)—call for additional information
Maximum Group	Up to 80, depending on types and ages of students
Group Notice	As much notice as possible
Eating Facilities	None
Restroom Facilities	Yes
Handicapped Access	No
Additional Information	Teachers are encouraged to bring cameras. Special programs done off-site for schools and groups.

Marine Nature Study Area
(Town of Hempstead)

THE MARINE NATURE Study Area is a 52-acre section of the Hempstead Estuary accessible to those who wish to learn about the environment of the marsh. Utmost care was taken not to disrupt the natural order, but visitors may take walking trails along which visual aids depict plant and animal communities.

Address/Telephone	500 Slice Drive Oceanside, NY 11572 766-1580
When to Visit	Monday to Sunday (April to October) Closed Saturdays (February and March) Closed Saturday, Sunday and holidays (November to January) 9:00 a.m. to 5:00 p.m.
Charges/Fees	None
Suggested Grades	5–Adult
Guided Tour	Yes, by arrangement
Maximum Group	75, with adequate supervision
Group Notice	As much notice as possible
Eating Facilities	None

Restroom Facilities	Yes
Handicapped Access	No, handicapped facilities limited to ramps only.
Additional Information	Call for information on programs and classroom visits.

Nassau County Fire Service Academy

THIS SERVICE ACADEMY is a specialized school in firefighting where Nassau County volunteer firefighters receive the latest and most scientific instruction in fire fighting and fire prevention. Visitors will see fire-fighting techniques in action.

Address/Telephone	Winding Road Old Bethpage, NY 11804 694-1234
When to Visit	Monday to Thursday May to October 7:30 p.m. to 9:30 p.m.
Charges/Fees	None
Suggested Grades	K–7
Guided Tour	Yes, 30 minutes
Maximum Group	30, with adequate supervision
Group Notice	1 month
Eating Facilities	None
Restroom Facilities	Yes
Handicapped Access	No
Additional Information	Most local fire departments offer tours and fire prevention programs.

Old Bethpage Village Restoration

THIS RESTORATION REPRESENTS a living-history museum that depicts the life of Long Island at mid-nineteenth century. The farm community includes a working blacksmith shop, a farmhouse, farm animals and other reminders of a way of life typical of old Long Island. The authentic homes, furnishings and active craftspeople, farmers and housewives recreate the lifestyle of a bygone era.

Old Bethpage Village Restoration

Address/Telephone	Round Swamp Road Old Bethpage, NY 11804 420-5288
When to Visit	Wednesday to Sunday December to February—10:00 a.m. to 4:00 p.m. March to November—10:00 a.m. to 5:00 p.m.
Charges/Fees	Adults—$5.00; Children—$3.00 Call for group rates
Suggested Grades	K–Adult
Guided Tour	2-hour self-guided tour
Maximum Group	30, with adequate supervision
Group Notice	1 month
Eating Facilities	Yes
Restroom Facilities	Yes
Handicapped Access	Yes
Additional Information	Appropriate attire for outdoors and walking. Operated by the Nassau County Department of Recreation and Parks.

Plaza Playhouse

PLAZA PLAYHOUSE IS a 260-seat, fully equipped, three-quarter-round playhouse specializing in fully staged musicals, comedies, children's theater and audience-participation murder mysteries. Typical productions are *My Fair Lady, Chapter Two, The Sound of Music, Arsenic and Old Lace, Little Shop of Horrors, Lend Me a Tenor, Gypsy* and *West Side Story*.

Address/Telephone	712 Old Bethpage Road Old Bethpage, NY 11804 694-3330
When to Visit	Adult public: Friday and Saturday—8:30 p.m.; Sunday—3:00 p.m. Children's theater: Saturday and Sunday—1:00 p.m. Audience participation murder mysteries: Thursday—8:00 p.m.

Schools and groups call for special schedule and rates.

Charges/Fees　$6.00–$18.00

Suggested Grades　Pre-K–Adult, depending on production

Guided Tour　None

Maximum Group　260

Group Notice　1 to 2 months

Eating Facilities　Yes, concession area

Restroom Facilities　Yes

Handicapped Access　Limited handicapped facilities—call for further information.

Additional Information　Arrangements can be made to meet the cast or staff and for wine and cheese parties.

New York Institute of Technology
(Fine Arts Department)

THE FINE ARTS Department features gallery exhibits in the areas of sculpture, photography, painting and graphics. These changing exhibits feature the work of talented faculty members, students and artists from outside the campus community.

Address/Telephone　New York Institute of Technology
268 Wheatly Road
Old Westbury, NY 11568
686-7542 Call: Fine Arts Dept.

When to Visit　Monday to Friday
September to June
9:00 a.m. to 5:00 p.m.

Charges/Fees　None

Suggested Grades　6–Adult

Guided Tour	None
Maximum Group	Unlimited
Group Notice	None
Eating Facilities	Yes, cafeterias on campus
Restroom Facilities	Yes
Handicapped Access	Yes

New York Institute of Technology
(Tours of Laboratories)

VISITORS WILL BE taken on a tour of the computer science laboratory, which offers some of the latest and most sophisticated systems available.

Address/Telephone	New York Institute of Technology 268 Wheatly Road Old Westbury, NY 11568 686-7549 Call: Mechanical Engineering Dept.
When to Visit	Monday to Friday September to May 9:00 a.m. to 5:00 p.m.
Charges/Fees	None
Suggested Grades	8–Adult
Guided Tour	Yes, up to 2 hours in length
Maximum Group	20, with 1 adult per group of 10
Group Notice	3 weeks
Eating Facilities	Yes, cafeteria
Restroom Facilities	Yes
Handicapped Access	Yes

New York Institute of Technology
(Tour of Radio and Television Studios)

THIS TRAINING FACILITY contains 2 color television studios, a video editing laboratory, a television newsroom, UPI wire service and state-of-the-art equipment in all areas. Also on premises are three radio laboratories equipped with modern stereo and mono consoles. A sound processing laboratory has voice recording and sound transfer and mixing facilities, including an 8-channel mixing board.

Address/Telephone	New York Institute of Technology
	268 Wheatly Road
	Old Westbury, NY 11568
	686-7567 Call: Communication Arts Dept.
When to Visit	Monday to Friday
	September to June
	9:00 a.m. to 4:30 p.m.
Charges/Fees	None
Suggested Grades	8–Adult
Guided Tour	Yes, 1 hour
Maximum Group	20, with 1 adult per group of 10
Group Notice	2 weeks
Eating Facilities	Yes, cafeteria
Restroom Facilities	Yes
Handicapped Access	Yes

New York Institute of Technology
(Water Pollution Control Plant)

VISITORS WILL OBSERVE the operation of a water pollution control plant utilizing primary and secondary sewage treatment. This plant processes liquid and scavenger wastes generated at the Institute.

Address/Telephone	New York Institute of Technology
	268 Wheatly Road
	Old Westbury, NY 11568
	686-7545 Call: Buildings and Grounds

When to Visit	Monday to Friday October to May 9:00 a.m. to 5:00 p.m.
Charges/Fees	None
Suggested Grades	8–Adult
Guided Tour	Yes, 30 to 60 minutes
Maximum Group	25, with 1 adult per group of 10
Group Notice	1 week
Eating Facilities	Yes, cafeteria
Restroom Facilities	Yes
Handicapped Access	No

Old Westbury Gardens

CONSTRUCTED AS A replica of an 18th-century English country estate, Old Westbury Gardens offers the visitor a view of the grandeur associated with Long Island, complete with a furnished mansion surrounded by formal gardens, open lawns and woodlands. Several small, contemporary gardens are planted to provide visitors with ideas and designs they may incorporate in their own gardens.

Old Westbury Gardens

Address/Telephone	71 Old Westbury Road Old Westbury, NY 11568 333-0048
When to Visit	Wednesday to Monday May to December 15 10:00 a.m. to 5:00 p.m.
Charges/Fees	Adults—Garden, $5.00; House, $3.00 Children—Garden, $2.50; House, $1.50 Seniors—Garden, $3.50; House, $1.50 Group Rates: 25 or more by arrangement
Suggested Grades	K–Adult
Guided Tour	Yes, house and garden, 2 hours
Maximum Group	Unlimited
Group Notice	6 weeks
Eating Facilities	Picnic facilities and snack bar
Restroom Facilities	Yes
Handicapped Access	Yes
Additional Information	Call for information regarding special educational guide provided during May and June. Multimedia available. Teacher syllabus available on request.

Coe Hall
(At Planting Fields Arboretum)

THIS TUDOR-STYLE mansion is a reminder of Long Island's Gold Coast of the 1920s. On display are fine European paintings and furnishings. Tours and programs should be of special interest to students studying architecture, art and history. Visitors are advised to make separate arrangements to visit Planting Fields Arboretum, the grounds on which the mansion is located.

Address/Telephone	*Planting Fields Road Oyster Bay, NY 11771 922-0479
When to Visit	February to November by appointment Special-interest groups can be accommodated in the morning by appointment

Coe Hall

Charges/Fees	Call for complete fee and program schedule
Suggested Grades	6–12
Guided Tour	Special program on "Architecture and Craftsmanship" as it relates to Coe Hall
Maximum Group	48 (minimum—14)
Group Notice	1 month
Eating Facilities	None
Restroom Facilities	Yes, limited
Handicapped Access	Yes
Additional Information	Due to newness of program, all visitors are advised to call. *Mailing address: Coe Hall, P.O. Box 58, Oyster Bay, NY 11771

Planting Fields Arboretum

THIS ARBORETUM WAS formerly the estate of William Robertson Coe. The house was replaced in 1921 after a fire, and is generally considered to be one of the finest examples of Elizabethan/Tudor architecture in America. About 160 acres are developed as an arboretum, which is comprised of thousands of ornamental trees and shrubs from around the world; 40 more acres are lawns, and the remaining 200 are preserved in their natural state. There are two large greenhouse ranges, one devoted to camellias—winter flowering December through March. The Main Greenhouse complex features economic plants of interest (bananas, citrus varieties, coffee, etc.) and collections of orchids, ferns, cacti and succulents, begonias, bromeliads, etc.

Address/Telephone	Planting Fields Road
	Oyster Bay, NY 11771
	922-9511
When to Visit	Monday to Sunday
	9:00 a.m. to 5:00 p.m.
	Greenhouses close at 4:30 p.m.
Charges/Fees	$3.00 parking fee daily from May 1 to Labor Day and on all holidays and weekends throughout the year.
	Schools call for group rates. Senior citizens free Monday to Friday with State pass.
Suggested Grades	K–Adult
Guided Tour	Call for appointment
Maximum Group	Unlimited
Group Notice	1 month
Eating Facilities	None
Restroom Facilities	Yes
Handicapped Access	Yes

Raynham Hall

DATING FROM 1740, this home of Samuel Townsend, whose son Robert was George Washington's chief spy in New York City, serves the town through a variety of programs. Included are a school program, summer programs and a lecture series for adults. On display are furnishings of the Colonial period plus a beautiful Christmas exhibit each December in the Victorian addition to the house.

Address/Telephone	20 West Main Street Oyster Bay, NY 11771 922-6808
When to Visit	Tuesday to Sunday 1:00 p.m. to 5:00 p.m. (self-tour) Morning hours for prearranged tours only
Charges/Fees	Adults—$2.00; children under 6—free Seniors and students over 6—$1.00
Suggested Grades	K–Adult
Guided Tour	Yes, by reservation only
Maximum Group	30, with 1 adult per group of 10
Group Notice	Call well in advance (for guided tour only)
Eating Facilities	None
Restroom Facilities	Yes
Handicapped Access	Only lower floor accessible
Additional Information	Craft and holiday workshops for children and adults by arrangement. Call for information on summer workshops. Multimedia available.

Theodore Roosevelt Sanctuary, Inc.

THE OLDEST NATIONAL Audubon Sanctuary in America, this sanctuary occupies 12 acres and is unique in that most of the trees, shrubs and vines were planted specifically to attract birds. The visitors' center displays information about the birds and plants, plus exhibits on Theodore Roosevelt and the Conservation Movement. The sanctuary offers workshops and courses for children and adults, conducts avian research and does wildlife rehabilitation for community members.

Address/Telephone	134 Cove Road Oyster Bay, NY 11771 922-3200
When to Visit	Monday to Sunday 9:00 a.m. to 5:00 p.m.
Charges/Fees	Free entrance Program—$2.00 per child
Suggested Grades	Pre-K–Adult
Guided Tour	Self-guided tour. Program and tour arranged for groups.
Maximum Group	30
Group Notice	2 weeks
Eating Facilities	None
Restroom Facilities	Yes
Handicapped Access	Yes
Additional Information	Education brochures and materials on request.

Sagamore Hill

SAGAMORE HILL WAS Theodore Roosevelt's permanent home and "summer White House" during his presidency. It contains the original furnishings and souvenirs from Roosevelt's travels to various countries. Most famous of this Victorian structure's 23 rooms is the North Room, which truly reflects the spirit of T. R. with its many hunting trophies, books, paintings, flags and furniture. Located on the same site is the Old Orchard Museum, home of Theodore Jr.

Address/Telephone	20 Sagamore Hill Road Oyster Bay, NY 11771 922-4447 or 922-4788
When to Visit	Monday to Sunday 9:30 a.m. to 5:00 p.m.

Theodore Roosevelt and family at Sagamore Hill

Charges/Fees	$1.00 per person—ages 17 to 61 School groups free by appointment
Suggested Grades	4–Adult
Guided Tour	Acoustiguide (cassette player) tour
Maximum Group	50, with 1 adult per group of 8
Group Notice	Call early in school year
Eating Facilities	Snack bar (summer only)
Restroom Facilities	Yes
Handicapped Access	Restrooms and first floor accessible to handicapped
Additional Information	Special film on Theodore Roosevelt at Old Orchard Museum—25 minutes.

The Townsend Museum

THIS LOVELY VICTORIAN house, built in 1890, is furnished with many of the pieces belonging to the family of Helen H. Townsend, who was a descendant of Henry Townsend, one of three brothers who came to Oyster Bay from Raynham, Norfolk, England.

Address/Telephone	107 E. Main Street
	Oyster Bay, NY 11771
	922-5434 or 671-0021
When to Visit	Saturday
	2:00 p.m. to 4:00 p.m.
Charges/Fees	$.50
Suggested Grades	Adults preferred
Guided Tour	Yes, 30 minutes or longer
Maximum Group	10 adults
Group Notice	1 week
Eating Facilities	None
Restroom Facilities	Yes
Handicapped Access	No

Wightman House
(Oyster Bay Historical Society)

FROM ITS ORIGINAL site on South Street, the Wightman House witnessed the American Revolution and the exciting role played in it by the Town of Oyster Bay. Built c. 1720, this historic landmark is furnished with period furniture. There is a reference library and changing historical exhibits.

Address/Telephone	*20 Summit Street
	Oyster Bay, NY 11771
	Schools—922-5800, ext. 2253
	Public—922-5032

When to Visit	Saturday 9:00 a.m. to 1:00 p.m. (Reference library only) Individuals and school groups by appointment— 922-6808
Charges/Fees	None
Suggested Grades	K–Adult
Guided Tour	Yes, program and slide presentation on Colonial life presented to schools and groups
Maximum Group	30, with adequate supervision
Group Notice	2 weeks
Eating Facilities	None
Restroom Facilities	Yes
Handicapped Access	Yes
Additional Information	*Mailing address: P.O. Box 297, Oyster Bay, NY 11771

WLIW
(Channel 21)

WLIW IS A public television station serving the residents of the tri-state area. Channel 21 is located in Plainview, along the border of Nassau and Suffolk Counties. Visitors will be given a tour of the production studio, master control, editing suites and tape library.

Address/Telephone	*Channel 21 Drive Plainview, NY 11803 367-2100
When to Visit	Write or call for appointment
Charges/Fees	None
Suggested Grades	7–Adult
Guided Tour	Yes, 30 minutes
Maximum Group	15
Group Notice	14 days

Eating Facilities	None
Restroom Facilities	Yes
Handicapped Access	Yes
Additional Information	*Mailing address: Public Information Dept., 1425 Old Country Road, P.O. Box 21, Plainview, NY 11803, Attn: Bob Trested

Polish-American Museum

THE POLISH-AMERICAN Museum features exhibits on Poles and Polish-Americans who have made valuable contributions to medicine, education, science, arts and political thought. Many paintings, drawings and pictures of Polish heros such as Generals Casimir Pulaski and Thaddeus Kosciuszko adorn the museum. A bilingual research library as well as historical documents and cultural artifacts are available for the use or observation of interested visitors.

Address/Telephone	16 Bellview Avenue Port Washington, NY 11050 883-6542
When to Visit	Monday to Friday—10:00 a.m. to 4:00 p.m. Saturday and Sunday—1:00 p.m. to 4:00 p.m.
Charges/Fees	Donation
Suggested Grades	4–Adult
Guided Tour	Yes, 60 to 90 minutes
Maximum Group	20
Group Notice	1 week
Eating Facilities	None
Restroom Facilities	Yes
Handicapped Access	No

Port Washington Water Pollution Control District

VISITORS WILL OBSERVE the operation of a water pollution control plant utilizing primary and secondary sewage treatment with sludge incineration. The final process of incineration permits total sterilization of sludge by-products, reduces volume and prevents the need to dump effluents in our coastal waters.

Address/Telephone	*70 Harbor Road Port Washington, NY 11050 944-6100
When to Visit	Fair-weather months only 10:00 a.m. to 3:00 p.m. By appointment
Charges/Fees	None
Suggested Grades	6–Adult
Guided Tour	Yes, 30 to 45 minutes
Maximum Group	20, with 3 adults
Group Notice	2 weeks
Eating Facilities	None
Restroom Facilities	None
Handicapped Access	No
Additional Information	*Mailing address: P.O. Box 790, Port Washington, NY 11050

Sands Point Preserve

THIS 216-ACRE PRESERVE is a former Gold Coast estate located on Long Island Sound. Once owned by the Gould and the Guggenheim families, these magnificent, castle-like buildings now house changing exhibits. "Falaise," the beautiful Normandy-style manor house owned by Harry Guggenheim and Alicia Patterson, which still holds all the family art and furnishings, is open for guided tours.

Address/Telephone	95 Middle Neck Road in Sands Point Park
	Port Washington, NY 11050
	Falaise: 883-1612
	Preserve: 883-1610
When to Visit	Tuesday to Sunday
	April to November
	Falaise closed Friday
Charges/Fees	Falaise tour: Ages 10 and up—$4.00; seniors—$3.00
	Call for group rates and arrangement
Suggested Grades	7–Adult
Guided Tour	Yes, 1 hour
Maximum Group	30
Group Notice	3 weeks
Eating Facilities	Picnic facilities
Restroom Facilities	Yes
Handicapped Access	Yes
Additional Information	No touching. Gift Shop. Operated by the Nassau Count Department of Recreation and Parks.

Sands-Willets House
(Cow Neck Peninsula Historical Society)

THE SANDS-WILLETS HOUSE presently serves as the Cow Neck Peninsula Historical Society's Museum. Featured are rooms and furnishings of the Colonial, Empire and Victorian periods. The original building which dates back to 1735 has a restored outer kitchen with a beehive oven and an open hearth fireplace for cooking and baking. A 1690 Dutch barn located on the property exhibits antique tools, carriages, local memorabilia and items owned by John Philip Sousa, resident of the area at one time. Exhibits will be changed.

Address/Telephone	336 Port Washington Boulevard
	Port Washington, NY 11050
	767-1447 Call: Mrs. Joslyn

When to Visit	Sunday April to December 2:00 p.m. to 4:00 p.m. Groups by appointment all year
Charges/Fees	Adults—$2.00; children—$1.00
Suggested Grades	K–Adult
Guided Tour	Yes, 90 minutes—call for information regarding group tours, lectures, and craft and cooking programs.
Maximum Group	30
Group Notice	1 month
Eating Facilities	None
Restroom Facilities	Yes
Handicapped Access	No
Additional Information	Caution around antiques

The Phillips House Museum

THE PHILLIPS HOUSE is one of the Victorian homes surviving from an era when influential, well-to-do sea captains lived in Rockville Centre. Built around 1882, the house blends the decorative style of the Victorian period with the classical simplicity found in New England cottages.

Address/Telephone	28 Hempstead Avenue Rockville Centre, NY 11570 678-9201
When to Visit	Saturday and Sunday 1:00 p.m. to 4:00 p.m. Weekdays by appointment Closed Saturday in July and August
Charges/Fees	None
Suggested Grades	K–Adult
Guided Tour	Yes, by appointment

Maximum Group	35
Group Notice	2 weeks
Eating Facilities	Picnic facilities
Restroom Facilities	Yes
Handicapped Access	No

Bryant Library Local History Collection

VISITORS MAY OBSERVE and use this specialized research collection, which includes the works of literary greats such as William Cullen Bryant and Christopher Morley. Also, many primary documents and works of local historians serve as part of the library's collection. First established in 1878, the library is the oldest continuing one on Long Island.

Address/Telephone	2 Paper Mill Road Roslyn, NY 11576 621-2240
When to Visit	Monday—9:00 a.m. to 5:00 p.m. Tuesday—9:00 a.m. to 9:00 p.m. Wednesday—10:00 a.m. to 5:30 p.m. Thursday and Friday—9:30 a.m. to 5:30 p.m. First Saturday of each month—9:00 a.m. to 5:00 p.m.
Charges/Fees	None
Suggested Grades	10–Adult
Guided Tour	By arrangement
Maximum Group	20
Group Notice	2 months
Eating Facilities	None
Restroom Facilities	Yes
Handicapped Access	No

Christopher Morley Knothole

MOVED FROM ITS original location "aloofly jungled as a Long Island suburb would permit," the Knothole is where Christopher Morley did much of his writing, including *Bartlett's Quotations* and bestseller *Kitty Foyle*. The cabin furnishings have been left unchanged and represent Morley's study as he himself used it.

Address/Telephone	Christopher Morley Park Searingtown Road Roslyn, NY 11576 621-9113
When to Visit	Call for schedule Groups by appointment
Charges/Fees	None
Suggested Grades	3–Adult
Guided Tour	Attendant on duty
Maximum Group	20
Group Notice	2 weeks
Eating Facilities	Yes, in park off center mall
Restroom Facilities	Yes
Handicapped Access	Yes
Additional Information	Operated by the Nassau County Department of Recreation and Parks

Nassau County Museum of Art

THE MUSEUM OCCUPIES the elegant neo-Georgian mansion of the Frick country estate, situated on 145 beautifully landscaped acres in the heart of Long Island's historic North Shore. Featuring ten refurbished galleries, the Museum produces four major art exhibitions per year. In addition, there are formal gardens, a unique trellis, ponds and a wildflower walk that provides a sequence of delightful vistas in which to enjoy nature and monumental outdoor sculpture.

Address/Telephone	*One Museum Drive (Off Northern Boulevard) Roslyn, NY 11576 484-9337 (Call for events information)
When to Visit	Tuesday to Sunday 11:00 a.m. to 5:00 p.m.
Charges/Fees	Adults—$3.00; children and seniors—$2.00 Free on Fridays.
Suggested Grades	K–Adult
Guided Tour	Free every Wednesday and Saturday at 2:00 p.m. or by appointment for groups
Maximum Group	50—by appointment
Group Notice	3 to 4 weeks
Eating Facilities	Museum café located in museum, serving light lunch from noon to 4:00 p.m., Tuesday to Sunday.
Restroom Facilities	Yes
Handicapped Access	Yes, special ramps and signage for handicapped persons
Additional Information	Museum Gift Shop offers many unusual and attractive items, including Museum replicas, jewelry and art-related stationery. Museum Bookstore offers a wide selection of art publications, posters and scholarly books for art students. Call Chris (484-9336) to ask about art classes for adults and children. *Mailing address: One Museum Dr., Roslyn Harbor, NY 11576

St. Francis Hospital
(The Heart Center)

VISITORS TO ST. FRANCIS Hospital will tour New York State's and Long Island's Heart Center. The visit will include tours of a number of the departments essential to both cardiac and noncardiac medicine.

Address/Telephone	100 Port Washington Boulevard Roslyn, NY 11576 562-6111

When to Visit	Monday to Friday
	10:00 a.m. to 3:00 p.m.
Charges/Fees	None
Suggested Grades	5–Adult
Guided Tour	Yes, 30 minutes
Maximum Group	15, with 2 adults
Group Notice	3 weeks
Eating Facilities	Yes, coffee shop
Restroom Facilities	Yes
Handicapped Access	Yes

Sea Cliff Village Museum
(Village of Sea Cliff)

THIS RELATIVELY NEW museum offers displays and information concerning the unique historical background of Sea Cliff. Included are photos, albums, documents, costumes, artifacts and various other memorabilia. An excellent place for reference, education and entertainment with regard to Sea Cliff Village.

Address/Telephone	95 Tenth Avenue
	Sea Cliff, NY 11579
	671-0090 or 671-0080
When to Visit	Weekends
	September to July
	2:00 p.m. to 5:00 p.m.
	Schools and groups by appointment
Charges/Fees	$1.00
Suggested Grades	K–Adult
Guided Tour	Yes, with slide program, 1 hour
Maximum Group	25
Group Notice	2 weeks
Eating Facilities	None
Restroom Facilities	Emergency only
Handicapped Access	No

Seaford Historical Society and Museum

T HE SEAFORD HISTORICAL Society and Museum, housed in a building built in 1893, once served as a two-room schoolhouse for the Seaford community and from 1919 to 1975 as a firehouse and community hall. The museum now contains many artifacts and memorabilia that reflect the farming and fishing life along the South Shore in the early days of the century, including tools, clothing, books, furniture and photos. Of special interest is a "Seaford skiff" built in 1906 and used by baymen to hunt and fish in the Great South Bay.

Address/Telephone	*3890 Waverly Avenue Seaford, NY 11783 735-9119 (afternoons and evenings) 826-1150
When to Visit	May to December Sunday—1:00 p.m. to 4:00 p.m. Wednesday—10:00 a.m. to 2:00 p.m. Schools and groups by appointment Other days and off-season by appointment
Charges/Fees	Donation
Suggested Grades	4–Adult
Guided Tour	Yes, 30 to 60 minutes
Maximum Group	35
Group Notice	1 week
Eating Facilities	None
Restroom Facilities	Yes
Handicapped Access	No
Additional Information	*Mailing address: Seaford Historical Society and Museum, 2234 Jackson Ave., Seaford, NY 11783

Takapausha Museum and Preserve

A REGIONAL MUSEUM of natural history, often referred to as the Life Sciences facility, it features exhibits depicting Long Island plant and animal life. An 80-acre preserve and 5 miles of nature trails adjoin the museum.

Address/Telephone	Washington Avenue Seaford, NY 11783 785-2802
When to Visit	Monday to Sunday Museum—10:00 a.m. to 4:45 p.m. Preserve—8:00 a.m. to sunset
Charges/Fees	Adults—$1.00; children 5 and over—$.50
Suggested Grades	K–Adult
Guided Tour	Yes, 1 hour
Maximum Group	30
Group Notice	Call for appointment
Eating Facilities	Picnic facilities
Restroom Facilities	Yes
Handicapped Access	Yes
Additional Information	Wear appropriate clothing and footwear for walking in preserve; tour given rain or shine. Collection of natural material is prohibited. Operated by the Nassau County Department of Recreation and Parks.

Town of Oyster Bay Animal Shelter

A T THIS PUBLIC shelter, visitors will learn how stray animals are picked up, how care is provided for them and how they, as well as abandoned animals, are relocated to new homes.

Address/Telephone	150 Miller Place Syosset, NY 11791 921-7731

When to Visit	Monday to Friday 10:00 a.m. to 2:00 p.m.
Charges/Fees	None
Suggested Grades	1 and up
Guided Tour	Yes, 15 to 25 minutes
Maximum Group	25
Group Notice	1 week
Eating Facilities	None
Restroom Facilities	Emergency only
Handicapped Access	Yes

Nassau Symphony Orchestra

THE FULLY PROFESSIONAL Nassau Symphony Orchestra annually presents a series of subscription concerts, both classics and pops, at Hofstra University's Adams Playhouse, SUNY Stony Brook's Staller Center, and other locations throughout Long Island, as well as its acclaimed "Music for Our Schools" educational programs, "Symphonies for Seniors," open dress rehearsals and many other concerts, recitals and programs for children, senior citizens, handicapped and underprivileged of the area.

Address/Telephone	Nassau Symphony Orchestra 185 California Avenue Uniondale, NY 11553-1131 481-3100 or 481-3196
When to Visit	Call for schedule
Charges/Fees	Call for information
Suggested Grades	4–Adult, depending on program
Guided Tour	Call for special school and senior citizen programs
Maximum Group	1,134 (at Hofstra, varies with location)
Group Notice	1 month
Eating Facilities	None
Restroom Facilities	Yes
Handicapped Access	Yes

Additional Information   Call for information on educational outreach programs involving Radio, TV and Orchestra
residencies.

Nassau Veterans Memorial Coliseum

B ILLED AS THE fifth-busiest building in America and home of hockey's
New York Islanders, the Nassau Veterans Memorial Coliseum
features sporting events, trade shows, concerts, family shows and other
forms of entertainment.

Address/Telephone	Nassau Veterans Memorial Coliseum
	1255 Hempstead Turnpike
	Uniondale, NY 11553-1200
	Attn: Group Sales
	794-9303
When to Visit	Varies with program
Charges/Fees	Varies with program
Suggested Grades	Pre-K–Adult
Guided Tour	None
Maximum Group	Unlimited (minimum eligible for group fee—25)
Group Notice	1 month or more depending on popularity
Eating Facilities	Yes
Restroom Facilities	Yes
Handicapped Access	Yes
Additional Information	Group sales office open Monday to Friday—
	9:00 a.m. to 5:00 p.m.

Jones Beach Theater

T HIS OPEN AMPHITHEATER, seating approximately 10,500 people, was
originally the Jones Beach Marine Theater. The theater is presently
undergoing a multi-million dollar redesign and reconstruction program.
While the original Marine Theater produced Broadway musicals, today it

is the site where musical groups perform in concert. Famous stars such as Frank Sinatra and Billy Joel have played and sung to capacity audiences at the Jones Beach Theater.

Address/Telephone	*Jones Beach State Park Wantagh, NY 11793 221-1000
When to Visit	July and August Monday to Saturday—10:00 a.m. to 6:00 p.m. Sunday—12:00 p.m. to 6:00 p.m. Shows: June to September
Charges/Fees	Write or call for season schedule
Suggested Grades	Varies with performance
Guided Tour	None
Maximum Group	Unlimited
Group Notice	As much as possible. Call as early as Memorial Day.
Eating Facilities	Yes
Restroom Facilities	Yes
Handicapped Access	Yes
Additional Information	*Mailing address: L.I. State Park and Recreation Commission, Belmont Lake State Park, Box 247, Babylon, NY 11702

Twin Lakes Preserve
(Town of Hempstead)

A S YOU WALK through this preserve you will become aware that the ponds are magnets for wildlife with their duckweed, water lilies and milfoil. Strolling through the woodlands and swamps, the visitor will observe sassafras, red maple, dogwood, sweetgum, black cherry and tupelo trees. Together, the plant life and pond water make the Twin Lakes Preserve a true wildlife habitat.

Address/Telephone	*Old Mill Road Wantagh, NY 11793 766-1580 or 221-1300
When to Visit	Monday to Sunday Dawn to dusk
Charges/Fees	None
Suggested Grades	5–Adult
Guided Tour	Yes, by arrangement (766-1580)
Maximum Group	50, with adequate supervision
Group Notice	As much as possible
Eating Facilities	None
Restroom Facilities	None
Handicapped Access	No
Additional Information	Call for information on naturalist-led tours and programs. *Mailing address: Marine Nature Study Area, 500 Slice Drive, Oceanside, NY 11572

Wantagh Preservation Society Museum

THIS MUSEUM IS housed in an 1885 railroad station and 1912 railroad parlor car. Together, in their restored states, they afford the visitor the opportunity to glimpse an important part of life at the turn of the century. Also on display are photographs depicting life in turn-of-the-century Wantagh.

Address/Telephone	Wantagh Avenue opposite Emerick Avenue P.O. Box 132 Wantagh, NY 11793 826-8767
When to Visit	April to November Sunday and Wednesday—1:00 p.m. to 4:00 p.m. December to March Sunday—2:00 p.m. to 4:00 p.m.

Charges/Fees	Donation
Suggested Grades	4–Adult
Guided Tour	Yes, by arrangement
Maximum Group	25
Group Notice	2 weeks
Eating Facilities	None
Restroom Facilities	Yes
Handicapped Access	No
Additional Information	Slide show available by arrangement.

Hempstead Resource Recovery, Inc.
(American Ref-Fuel)

VISITORS WILL OBSERVE the latest technology in solid waste resource recovery. This facility, which is New York's largest waste-to-energy plant, transfers municipal solid waste into electricity. Enough electricity is produced at this plant to supply the electrical energy needs for 65,000 suburban homes. Metals are recovered from the ash by-product and marketed.

Address/Telephone	600 Avenue C
	Westbury, NY 11590
	222-1050 Call: Mr. Raylman
When to Visit	By appointment
Charges/Fees	None
Suggested Grades	7–Adult
Guided Tour	Yes, 1 hour
Maximum Group	30, with 1 adult per group of 10
Group Notice	1 month
Eating Facilities	None
Restroom Facilities	Yes
Handicapped Access	No
Additional Information	Published information furnished upon request.

Hicks Nurseries, Inc.

THIS NURSERY DOES more than just sell the traditional plants, tools and nursery supplies. During the holiday season, displays are set up depicting a theme or story. Animated displays bring fairy tales to life as visitors walk among the various scenes. Halloween offers apples and pumpkins for sale. Christmas brings Santa Claus along with all the traditional animals associated with the holiday. Springtime, the most colorful of all seasons, brings flowers of all varieties for the visitor to observe or purchase for home or garden ornaments.

Address/Telephone	Jericho Turnpike Westbury, NY 11590 334-0066
When to Visit	Halloween Season—September 15 to November 1 Christmas Season—November 15 to December 26 Spring Season—March 1 to July 1 8:00 a.m. to 6:00 p.m.
Charges/Fees	None
Suggested Grades	K–7
Guided Tour	None
Maximum Group	100, with 1 adult per group of 5
Group Notice	3 days
Eating Facilities	None
Restroom Facilities	Yes
Handicapped Access	Yes

Westbury Music Fair

OFFERING THE ONLY example of a professional theater-in-the-round in the metropolitan area, Westbury Music Fair features a variety of plays, musicals and concerts. Scheduled throughout the year during holidays and summertime are full-scale productions designed to appeal to children such as *Peter Rabbit*, *Raggedy Ann and Andy*, *Hansel and Gretel* and *Goldilocks and the Three Bears*.

Address/Telephone	Brush Hollow Road
	Westbury, NY 11590
	334-0800—General Box Office
	333-2101—Group Information (Mrs. Kramer)
When to Visit	Write or call for schedule
Charges/Fees	Varies with program
Suggested Grades	All ages—depending on program
Guided Tour	None
Maximum Group	2,870
Group Notice	Early as possible, depending on popularity of program
Eating Facilities	Yes
Restroom Facilities	Yes
Handicapped Access	Yes

SUFFOLK COUNTY

The Amelia Cottage Museum
(Amagansett Historical Association)

BUILT IN 1725 and moved to its present site in 1794, the museum displays furnishings from many periods of history, but especially a fine collection of Dominy furniture. Featuring a unique divided staircase, the cottage also boasts much of the original knife-and-groove paneling as well as iron, hand-wrought hinges and outer hardware, and a huge fireplace.

Address/Telephone	Montauk Highway and Windmill Lane
	Amagansett, NY 11930
	267-6835
When to Visit	Friday to Sunday
	1:00 p.m. to 5:00 p.m.
Charges/Fees	Adults—$2.00; children—$1.00
Suggested Grades	K–Adult
Guided Tour	None, curator on duty
Maximum Group	30, with one adult per group of 15
Group Notice	10 days
Eating Facilities	None
Restroom Facilities	Yes
Handicapped Access	No

East Hampton Town Marine Museum
(East Hampton Historical Society)

L OCATED ON 36 acres overlooking the sea, this museum displays, in
interpretive exhibits, artifacts and descriptions of the traditions and
working life of local fishermen. Through them one traces the development of the fishing and whaling industries of the past three centuries and
learns the lore and technology of boating for work and for leisure.

Address/Telephone	Atlantic Avenue and Bluff Road
	Amagansett, NY 11930
	267-6544
When to Visit	Saturday and Sunday—June and September
	Daily—July 4 to Labor Day
	10:00 a.m. to 5:00 p.m.
	Groups call for appointment during season and
	winter months
Charges/Fees	Adults—$2.00; children—$1.00; seniors—$1.50
	Please call for discounted group rates
Suggested Grades	K–Adult
Guided Tour	None
Maximum Group	40, with adequate supervision
Group Notice	1 week
Eating Facilities	Picnic facilities
Restroom Facilities	Yes
Handicapped Access	No

The Roy K. Lester Carriage Museum
(Amagansett Historical Association)

A COLLECTION OF 27 carriages displayed in two large barns, ranging
from delicate buggies and elegant formal carriages to a full-size
replica of a Heavy Concord Stagecoach. These vehicles are a wonderful
marriage of art and engineering, utility and elegance. The collection

brings back to life a form of transportation that was predominant for many years. Some of the carriages have been fully restored, but most are in original condition.

Address/Telephone	Montauk Highway and Windmill Lane Amagansett, NY 11930 267-6835
When to Visit	Friday to Sunday 1:00 p.m. to 5:00 p.m.
Charges/Fees	Adults—$2.00; children—$1.00
Suggested Grades	K–Adult
Guided Tour	None, curator on duty
Maximum Group	30, with one adult per group of 15
Group Notice	10 days
Eating Facilities	None
Restroom Facilities	Yes
Handicapped Access	Yes

Lauder Museum
(Amityville Historical Society)

THIS MUSEUM, ONCE the Bank of Amityville, serves as the attractive home for memorabilia of Amityville's past. Here this material is collected, preserved and exhibited. It is also from this point that a self-guided historical walking tour of Amityville begins.

Address/Telephone	170 Broadway and Ireland Place Amityville, NY 11701 598-1486
When to Visit	Tuesday, Friday and Sunday 2:00 p.m. to 4:00 p.m. Groups on Tuesday and Friday by appointment
Charges/Fees	None
Suggested Grades	1–9
Guided Tour	Yes, 1 hour by arrangement
Maximum Group	30, with 1 adult per group of 10

Group Notice	2 weeks
Eating Facilities	None
Restroom Facilities	Yes
Handicapped Access	Ramp for handicapped

Wilderness Traveling Museum

THE WILDERNESS TRAVELING Museum is the field trip that comes to you and provides hands-on learning experience with Native American culture and natural history understanding. The Museum offers in-school programs for children three years old and up, which can be tailored to the particular needs of your children.

Address/Telephone	P.O. Box 88
	Peconic Bay Boulevard
	Aquebogue, NY 11931
	722-4645
When to Visit	By appointment
Charges/Fees	Varies with program
Suggested Grades	Pre-K–Adult
Guided Tour	Yes, by appointment
Maximum Group	By arrangement
Group Notice	1 to 2 months
Eating Facilities	According to location
Restroom Facilities	According to location
Handicapped Access	May vary according to location

Eaton's Neck Coast Guard Station and Lighthouse

THIS COAST GUARD station serves as a base for search and rescue operations. A communications center, weather observation post, boats and lighthouse are part of the facility. The tour includes the main building and a close-up view of the boats. Visitors will have a chance to meet the personnel, see and hear the radios in operation and hear an explanation of the rescue process. Other areas of the station's responsibility include Law Enforcement and Marine Pollution Investigation.

Address/Telephone	*Ocean Avenue to Eaton's Neck to Lighthouse Road Asharokan, NY 11768 261-6868 Call: Commanding Officer
When to Visit	Not open to the general public; groups only, by appointment 9:00 a.m. to 11:00 a.m. and 1:00 p.m. to 4:00 p.m.
Charges/Fees	None
Suggested Grades	2–Adult
Guided Tour	Yes, 45 minutes
Maximum Group	30, with adequate supervision
Group Notice	1 week
Eating Facilities	None
Restroom Facilities	Emergency only
Handicapped Access	No
Additional Information	*Mailing address: Northport, NY 11768

Great South Bay Cruises and Excursions
(Captree Spray and Moonchaser)

THE CAPTREE SPRAY and the Moonchaser offer groups and the general public the opportunity to enjoy the picturesque scenery surrounding Great South Bay. Fully equipped with an enclosed maindeck and canopied upper sun deck, both vessels offer comfort and enjoyment whether used for a general excursion or catered affair. A variety of cruises and experiences are offered or may be specially arranged.

Address/Telephone	*Captree State Park Captree Boat Basin Babylon, NY 11702 661-5061

When to Visit	Daily
	May to October
	Call for arrangements
Charges/Fees	Call for information
Suggested Grades	Pre-K–Adult
Guided Tour	None
Maximum Group	250 per boat
Group Notice	Advance notice advised
Eating Facilities	Beverages available—"brown bag"
Restroom Facilities	Yes
Handicapped Access	Yes
Additional Information	Dinner cruises to Fire Island. Excursions from July 4 to Labor Day.
	*Mailing address: P.O. Box 204, West Islip, NY 11795

Village of Babylon Historical and Preservation Society

HOUSED IN A building that was formerly the Babylon Village Library, this museum contains artifacts, photographs and memorabilia relative to Babylon and West Islip history. There is an old horsedrawn carriage, a pony cart, textiles, quilts, clothing, antique farming tools, a blacksmith's bellows and a grassboat with decoys. Also displayed are old toys and home items such as a butter churn and sewing machine. In addition, there are exhibits that change periodically.

Address/Telephone	117 W. Main Street
	Babylon, NY 11702
	669-7086
When to Visit	Tuesday and Saturday
	2:00 p.m. to 4:00 p.m.
	Groups by appointment
Charges/Fees	Donation

Suggested Grades	3–Adult
Guided Tour	None
Maximum Group	25, with adequate supervision
Group Notice	1 week
Eating Facilities	None
Restroom Facilities	Yes
Handicapped Access	No
Additional Information	School-term history tour of Babylon Village available for school groups. Call for arrangements.

Bayport Aerodrome Society Museum

THE BAYPORT AERODROME Society is a membership organization formed in 1972 for the primary purpose of preserving the style and tradition of aviation in the early 20th century (together with the turf airfield at Bayport, New York). Since its formation, the Society has built 24 hangars housing antique and classic aircraft from Aeroncas to Wacos. The Society has also created a Museum Hangar for aircraft display and exhibitions. This hangar is fully heated and also houses the meeting area and library.

Address/Telephone	*Cartwright Loop off Church Street Bayport, NY 11705 585-9214—Leave message 277-2229—Leave message
When to Visit	All visits by appointment only 1st and 3rd Sunday of the month 10:00 a.m. to 4:00 p.m. Other times by special arrangement
Charges/Fees	None
Suggested Grades	K–Adult
Guided Tour	Yes, 30 minutes
Maximum Group	15

Group Notice	1 week
Eating Facilities	None
Restroom Facilities	Yes
Handicapped Access	No
Additional Information	*Mailing address: P.O. Box 728, Bayport, NY 11705

Antique Doll House Museum

THIS INTERESTING COLLECTION, turned into a museum, features almost 5,000 dolls. The wide variety of dolls, and particularly the antique and ethnic dolls, spark the interest of both young and older visitors. Also featured are antique doll houses, toys and miniatures.

Address/Telephone	17 Sunset Road Bay Shore, NY 11706 666-6847
When to Visit	By appointment
Charges/Fees	Adults—$2.00; children under 12—free
Suggested Grades	K–Adult
Guided Tour	Yes, 90 minutes
Maximum Group	30
Group Notice	10 days
Eating Facilities	None
Restroom Facilities	Yes
Handicapped Access	No

Southside Hospital

THIS VOLUNTARY, NONPROFIT community hospital offers tours of the Radiology Department, Laboratory, Computer Center and other facilities. The day-to-day operations of a modern hospital will be observed by visitors.

Address/Telephone	Montauk Highway Bay Shore, NY 11706 968-3477
When to Visit	Monday to Friday 9:00 a.m. to 5:00 p.m. Other hours by appointment
Charges/Fees	None
Suggested Grades	8–Adult
Guided Tour	Yes, 1 hour
Maximum Group	15, with 2 adults
Group Notice	3 weeks
Eating Facilities	Yes
Restroom Facilities	Yes
Handicapped Access	Yes
Additional Information	Call for special dates and accommodations for larger groups.

Bellport-Brookhaven Historical Society Barn Museum Complex

A VISIT TO THIS museum complex offers exhibits on marine life, Indian artifacts and toys. Farm tools are on display, while the Exchange Shop features small antiques, old silver, pattern and cut glass and prints and paintings by area artists. Also exhibited are decoys, weapons and textiles and fully equipped shop, milkhouse and studio museum of early American decoration.

Address/Telephone	12 Bell Street and 31 Bellport Lane Bellport, NY 11713 286-0888
When to Visit	Thursday to Saturday Memorial Day to Labor Day 1:00 p.m. to 4:30 p.m.

Charges/Fees	Adults—$1.00; children—$.50
Suggested Grades	1–Adult
Guided Tour	Yes, 30 to 60 minutes
Maximum Group	30, with adequate supervision
Group Notice	1 week
Eating Facilities	Yes, nearby
Restroom Facilities	Yes
Handicapped Access	No
Additional Information	Gift shop open Wednesday to Saturday—11:00 a.m. to 5:00 p.m., Memorial Day to December 19th.

Airport Playhouse

THE AIRPORT PLAYHOUSE is a year-round professional theater now entering its fifteenth year. In addition to its annual roster of ten full-scale productions, the Playhouse also offers an innovative "Tuesday at 8:00" series and year-round Children's Theatre. Typical of a season's productions are *The Music Man*, *Noises Off* and *St. Louis Blues*.

Address/Telephone	*Knickerbocker Avenue Bohemia, NY 11716 589-7588
When to Visit	Wednesday—8:00 p.m. Friday and Saturday—9:00 p.m. Sunday—7:30 p.m. Call for schedule of children's and matinee performances
Charges/Fees	Call for most recent schedule
Suggested Grades	Pre-K–Adult, depending on production
Guided Tour	None
Maximum Group	279
Group Notice	2 weeks
Eating Facilities	Concession and liquid refreshments on premises

Restroom Facilities	Yes
Handicapped Access	No
Additional Information	*Mailing address: P.O. Box 162, Bohemia, NY 11716-0162

Bridgehampton Winery

T HE BRIDGEHAMPTON WINERY is proud to announce the opening of the first bonded winery of the Hamptons. It is currently producing two fine white wines, the Bridgehampton Chardonnay and Riesling. Upon visiting the winery one will have the opportunity to sample and learn about the production of these two wines. From the deck you can view the beautiful vineyards and enjoy the usually pleasant weather. With over 100 awards and medals garnered on the international, national and state fronts, Bridgehampton has achieved much success with its European-styled Chardonnays and Merlot.

Address/Telephone	*Sag Harbor Turnpike Bridgehampton, NY 11932 537-3155
When to Visit	Daily March to November 11:00 a.m. to 5:00 p.m.
Charges/Fees	$2.00
Suggested Grades	5–Adult
Guided Tour	Yes, 45 minutes
Maximum Group	45
Group Notice	1 week
Eating Facilities	None
Restroom Facilities	Yes
Handicapped Access	No
Additional Information	*Mailing address: Box 979, Bridgehampton, NY 11932

Corwith Homestead
(Bridgehampton Historical Society)

THE OLD HOMESTEAD, now a museum, has Colonial, Empire and Victorian furnishings. On display are operating antique engines, tractors and other farm machines, which are actually run for the public at a fair during the end of August. Also on site are the Egbert Howell Hildreth Barn, the George W. Strong Wheelwright Shop and an old jail.

Address/Telephone	Montauk Highway
	Bridgehampton, NY 11932
	537-1088 or 537-0601
When to Visit	Thursday, Friday and Saturday
	mid-June to September 1
	Noon to 4:00 p.m.
	Groups by appointment
Charges/Fees	Donation
Suggested Grades	3–Adult
Guided Tour	Yes, 30 minutes to 1 hour
Maximum Group	20
Group Notice	2 weeks
Eating Facilities	None
Restroom Facilities	None
Handicapped Access	No

DIA Center for the Arts

THE INSTITUTE IS located in the renovated local Hook and Ladder Co. No. 1 (1908) and First Baptist Church Building (1924). It exhibits historical and contemporary works of art, often of Long Island interest.

Address/Telephone	Corwith Avenue
	Bridgehampton, NY 11932
	537-1476

When to Visit	Thursday to Sunday
	Memorial Day to September
	Noon to 6:00 p.m.
Charges/Fees	None
Suggested Grades	9–Adult
Guided Tour	None
Maximum Group	50
Group Notice	Arrange in advance
Eating Facilities	None
Restroom Facilities	Yes
Handicapped Access	No

Canoe the Carmans River
(Carmans River Canoe)

THE CARMANS RIVER trip begins at Mill Road, across the highway from Upper Lake in Yaphank. The river is very narrow and extremely shrouded with forest cover where the canoes enter the water. Navigating the waterway is rather tight and difficult until Lower Lake is reached. A portage across Yaphank Road from the lake brings canoers into South Haven County Park for the remainder of the trip. This river offers some of the most pristine wilderness along Suffolk's three major rivers. The trip terminates at the boating and duck pond at the southern border of the park.

Address/Telephone	2979 Montauk Highway
	Brookhaven, NY 11719
	286-1966
When to Visit	March 31 to November 15
	Monday to Friday—9:00 a.m. to 5:00 p.m.
	Saturday and Sunday—8:00 a.m. to 5:00 p.m.
Charges/Fees	$28.00—single kayak
	$40.00—double kayak
	$30.00—one canoe
	Call for group rates
	Reservation required for group (call for information)

Suggested Grades　K–Adult—adequate supervision mandatory

Guided Tour　Map of river provided

Maximum Group　Call for information

Group Notice　1 week

Eating Facilities　Call for information

Restroom Facilities　Yes

Handicapped Access　No

Additional Information　Life jackets and paddles provided
A-Trip: Leave car at South Haven Park Terminus, transport of Lower Lake.
B-Trip: Leave car at Carmans River Canoe and paddle through Wertheim Refuge.

Kids for Kids Productions, Inc.

THIS ORGANIZATION, WHICH is designed to train young people in all aspects of the theater, presents professional performances to the public at local theaters as well as sending a touring company to your own theater. Workshop sessions emphasizing skill development in drama, voice, movement, dance and technical theater are also available.

Address/Telephone　Middle Country School District
Unity Drive Learning Center
Centereach, NY 11720
737-0011

When to Visit　Call or write for schedule

Charges/Fees　All tickets—$6.00, groups—$4.50
Senior citizens—$4.00

Suggested Grades　Pre-K–Adult

Guided Tour　By arrangement

Maximum Group　500

Group Notice　2 to 4 weeks

Eating Facilities　None

Restroom Facilities	Yes
Handicapped Access	No
Additional Information	Touring company available to perform at your theater or school. Workshops on theater skills for youngsters age 4–10. Free performances available for nursing homes, hospitals and charitable organizations.

Haven's House

THE HAVEN'S HOUSE, which serves as the headquarters for the Moriches Bay Historical Society, was first built in 1740. Essentially a farmhouse, a Victorian section was added in 1900. The museum displays many items of local memorabilia, Indian artifacts, military medals and 19th-century clothing. Also located at the Haven's House is a library containing various volumes on local and Long Island history.

Address/Telephone	*Montauk Highway and Chet Sweezy Road Center Moriches, NY 11934 878-1776
When to Visit	Saturday 10:00 a.m. to 5:00 p.m. Groups by appointment
Charges/Fees	None
Suggested Grades	3–Adult
Guided Tour	Yes, 1 hour
Maximum Group	25
Group Notice	1 week
Eating Facilities	None
Restroom Facilities	Emergency only
Handicapped Access	No
Additional Information	*Mailing address: P.O. Box 31, Center Moriches, NY 11934

The Barn Museum
(Greenlawn-Centerport Historical Association)

THE BARN MUSEUM contains a farm workshop, farm wagon and tool exhibit. There is an upstairs gallery housing home furnishings (including quilts) from 19th-century houses in the area.

Address/Telephone	1 Fort Salonga Road Centerport, NY 11721 754-1180
When to Visit	Sunday May to October 1:00 p.m. to 4:00 p.m.
Charges/Fees	None
Suggested Grades	4–Adult
Guided Tour	Yes, call for further information
Maximum Group	25
Group Notice	3 weeks
Eating Facilities	None
Restroom Facilities	Yes
Handicapped Access	No

Vanderbilt Mansion and Marine Museum

THIS 43-ACRE ESTATE, with gardens, Spanish-style mansion and a museum, overlooks picturesque Northport Harbor and Long Island Sound. Given to Suffolk County by William K. Vanderbilt II, it contains original furnishings from the Vanderbilt years, including carved marble and wood fireplaces, elaborate ceilings and marble-clad galleries. Also on display are wildlife dioramas and exhibits of science and natural history created by Mr. Vanderbilt with collections from his family's travel to exotic places. The Marine Museum is a separate building that houses over 2,000 specimens of marine biology.

Vanderbilt Mansion and Marine Museum

OSCAR SHOENFELD

Address/Telephone	Little Neck Road Centerport, NY 11721 262-7800
When to Visit	November to February: Tuesday to Saturday—Noon to 4:00 p.m. March to October: Tuesday to Saturday—10:00 a.m. to 4:00 p.m. All year (in addition): Sunday—Noon to 5:00 p.m.

Charges/Fees	General Admission: Adults—$5.00; students and seniors—$3.00; children—$1.00 All-House Guided Tours—$3.00 All-Day Sky Shows—$3.00 Night Sky Shows: Adults—$5.00; students and seniors—$4.00; children—$2.50
Suggested Grades	K–Adult
Guided Tour	Yes, 1 hour
Maximum Group	By arrangement
Group Notice	1 week
Eating Facilities	Outdoor picnic area
Restroom Facilities	Yes
Handicapped Access	No
Additional Information	Gift shop

Vanderbilt Planetarium

THE VANDERBILT MUSEUM Planetarium is one of the largest and best equipped in the United States. It can show the sun, moon, stars and planets in various configurations for any time period. Images of snow, rain, meteor showers and spacewalkers appear on the 60-foot dome. On clear evenings when public shows are scheduled, an observatory with a 16-inch Cassegrainian reflecting telescope is also open.

Address/Telephone	Little Neck Road Centerport, NY 11721 Recorded message—262-STAR Office—262-7800
When to Visit	Call for schedule
Charges/Fees	Adults—$5.00; students and seniors—$4.00; children under 12—$2.50
Suggested Grades	1–Adult
Guided Tour	None
Maximum Group	238

Group Notice	Varies with program—call at least 1 week in advance
Eating Facilities	Outdoor picnic area
Restroom Facilities	Yes
Handicapped Access	No
Additional Information	Observe the rules and regulations. No cameras in the planetarium. Written information available on request.

Cold Spring Harbor Whaling Museum

THIS MUSEUM'S ROOMS are filled with hundreds of items evoking memories of the whaling era, including a fully rigged whale boat, scrimshaw, whaling tools and a diorama of Cold Spring Harbor in its whaling port days. The museum offers programs and workshops in scrimshaw, crafts and sea chanteys and a "hands-on" whalebone display. There are special events scheduled on Sunday afternoons. Call for schedule.

Address	*Main Street (Route 25A) Cold Spring Harbor, NY 11724
When to Visit	Daily (Memorial Day to Labor Day) Tuesday to Sunday (September to May) 11:00 a.m. to 5:00 p.m.
Charges/Fees	Adults—$2.00; seniors—$1.50; children (6–14)—$1.00
Suggested Grades	Pre-K–Adult
Guided Tour	By arrangement (1 hour with slides or film presentation)
Maximum Group	30 (school groups can be larger)
Group Notice	1 month
Eating Facilities	None
Restroom Facilities	Yes
Handicapped Access	Yes, ramp for handicapped
Additional Information	*Mailing address: P.O. Box 25, Cold Spring Harbor, NY 11724

DNA Learning Center

DNA Learning Center
(Cold Spring Harbor Laboratory)

THE DNA LEARNING CENTER is a unique educational resource—the nation's first facility dedicated to improving DNA science education. In the modern Bio2000 Teaching Laboratory, the Learning Center staff stresses an interactive approach linking the process of discovery to learning. The Center also maintains a museum program and hosts various and changing exhibits.

Address/Telephone   334 Main Street
Cold Spring Harbor, NY 11724
367-7240

When to Visit	Tuesday to Saturday 10:00 a.m. to 4:00 p.m.
Charges/Fees	General admission—$3.00; students and seniors— $2.00; children under 13—free Call for group rates and program fees
Suggested Grades	7–Adult
Guided Tour	Self-guided
Maximum Group	By arrangement
Group Notice	2 weeks
Eating Facilities	None
Restroom Facilities	Yes
Handicapped Access	Yes
Additional Information	Special programs available for middle and high schools. Call for arrangements.

The Gallery
(Society for the Preservation of Long Island Antiquities)

LOCATED AT ONE end of the picturesque Village of Cold Spring Harbor, the Gallery provides an opportunity through changing exhibitions to explore aspects of Long Island's distinctive social and cultural history. The Gallery's Museum Shop features an excellent collection of books and objects related to Long Island.

Address	Main Street and Shore Road Cold Spring Harbor, NY 11724
When to Visit	Thursday to Sunday (January to April) Tuesday to Sunday (May to December) 11:00 a.m. to 4:00 p.m.
Charges/Fees	Adults—$1.50; children and seniors—$1.00
Suggested Grades	2–Adult
Guided Tour	Available by appointment

Maximum Group	By arrangement
Group Notice	2 weeks
Eating Facilities	None
Restroom Facilities	Yes
Handicapped Access	No
Additional Information	Brochure available

Uplands Farm Sanctuary
(The Nature Conservancy)

THE HEADQUARTERS OF the Long Island Chapter of The Nature Conservancy, this area of open fields, ash and oak hedgerows, upland woods and farm buildings is also home for the Uplands Farm Sanctuary. The Chapter offers a reference library and small gift shop. A detailed guide is available to lead one through the trails of Uplands.

Address/Telephone	*Lawrence Hill Road Cold Spring Harbor, NY 11724 367-3225 or 367-3281
When to Visit	Monday to Friday—8:00 a.m. to 4:00 p.m Monday to Sunday—sunrise to sunset (Sanctuary use only)
Charges/Fees	None
Suggested Grades	3–Adult
Guided Tour	Self-guided trails
Maximum Group	50, with adequate supervision
Group Notice	2 weeks
Eating Facilities	None
Restroom Facilities	Yes, Monday to Friday, 8:00 a.m. to 4:00 p.m. only
Handicapped Access	No
Additional Information	*Mailing address: c/o The Nature Conservancy, 250 Lawrence Hill Road, Cold Spring Harbor, NY 11724

Hoyt Farm Nature Center
(Town of Smithtown)

THE HOYT FARM Nature Center is a 133-acre multiple-use park and wildlife preserve. A nature trail with 33 stops has been designed to show all of the habitats and their inhabitants that are to be found at the Farm. A nature center offers exhibits on the natural history of Long Island. A section of the Hoyt house is devoted to a historical museum featuring furniture and artifacts representing late 18th-century through early 20th-century rural life on Long Island. Visitors will also find a farm animal complex with live animals.

Address/Telephone	New Highway Commack, NY 11725 543-7804
When to Visit	Memorial Day to September Hoyt House: Saturday and Sunday—2:00 p.m. to 5:00 p.m. Nature Center: Daily—12:00 p.m. to 5:00 p.m. Park: All year—8:00 a.m. to dusk School and youth groups by appointment only
Charges/Fees	Fee for educational programs only
Suggested Grades	2–Adult
Guided Tour	Program and tour, 1 hour
Maximum Group	30
Group Notice	2 weeks
Eating Facilities	Picnic facilities
Restroom Facilities	Yes
Handicapped Access	Limited handicapped facilities available
Additional Information	Environmental education programs by arrangement throughout the year.

Telephone Pioneers Museum

Telephone Pioneers Museum
(Paumanok Chapter of the Telephone Pioneers of America Historical Museum)

THIS MUSEUM HOUSES nearly 150 phones of all shapes and sizes. In addition, there are nine display units, each with internal lighting and a taped message depicting such things as a lineman explaining how he does the wiring on a telephone pole and a handcrank phone that narrates its history. The museum also contains a rare letter written by Thomas Watson (Bell's co-worker), plus a collection of old telephone directories and an 1893 telephone annual report.

Address/Telephone	445 Commack Road
	Commack, NY 11725
	543-1321
When to Visit	Daily—9:30 a.m. to 4:00 p.m. (By appointment only)
	First Sunday of each month—1:00 p.m. to 4:00 p.m. (open house, no appointment needed)
Charges/Fees	None
Suggested Grades	2–Adult
Guided Tour	Yes, 1 hour
Maximum Group	50, with 4 adults
Group Notice	2 weeks
Eating Facilities	None
Restroom Facilities	Yes
Handicapped Access	Yes

Bedell Cellars

VISITORS TO BEDELL Cellars are given the opportunity to sample award-winning Merlot, Chardonnay and Cabernet Sauvignon wines in a barnlike structure that overlooks the 28-acre vineyard. Aside from a visit to the tasting room, tours are given through the fields and winery as well for groups of 10 or more.

Address/Telephone	Main Road (Route 25)
	Cutchogue, NY 11935
	734-7537
When to Visit	Daily
	11:00 a.m. to 5:00 p.m.
Charges/Fees	None
Suggested Grades	K–Adult

Guided Tour	For groups (10 or more)
Maximum Group	30
Group Notice	1 week
Eating Facilities	Picnic facilities available
Restroom Facilities	Yes
Handicapped Access	Yes

Bidwell Vineyards

SITUATED IN THE heart of Long Island wine country, Bidwell Vineyards has distinguished itself by producing a number of award-winning wines. Five specific varieties of grapes are grown to produce seven types of wine. Tours and tasting experiences are offered to visitors on an hourly basis.

Address/Telephone	Route 48 Cutchogue, NY 11935 734-5200
When to Visit	Daily 11:00 a.m. to 6:00 p.m. Last tour: 5:00 p.m.
Charges/Fees	None
Suggested Grades	9–Adult
Guided Tour	Yes
Maximum Group	40
Group Notice	2 weeks
Eating Facilities	Picnic facilities
Restroom Facilities	Yes
Handicapped Access	No
Additional Information	Call for special events and program calendar

Hargrave Vineyard

A T THE HARGRAVE Vineyard the visitor will see (depending on the time of year) the grapes growing on the vines and the pickers at work harvesting them. There is also a wine cellar, barrel-aging room and a wine-tasting room.

Address/Telephone	Alvah's Lane and Route 48 Cutchogue, NY 11935 734-5158
When to Visit	Daily—11:00 a.m. to 5:00 p.m. (May to October) (Tours—3:00 p.m.) Saturday and Sunday—11:00 a.m. to 5:00 p.m. (November to December) (Tours—2:00 p.m.)
Charges/Fees	None
Suggested Grades	No youth or school groups
Guided Tour	Yes, 1-hour groups only by arrangement
Maximum Group	30
Group Notice	1 week
Eating Facilities	None
Restroom Facilities	Yes
Handicapped Access	No
Additional Information	Call for holiday schedule and special events.

Peconic Bay Vineyards

P ECONIC BAY VINEYARDS are located on the site of a century-old potato farm. Today, this mature grape vineyard produces grapes for five traditional European varieties of wine. The public is invited to daily wine-tasting sessions from April through December.

Address/Telephone	Main Road—Route 25 Cutchogue, NY 11935 734-7361

When to Visit	Daily—April to December
	Friday to Sunday—January to March
	11:00 a.m. to 5:00 p.m.
Charges/Fees	None
Suggested Grades	K–Adult
Guided Tour	None
Maximum Group	20
Group Notice	Call ahead
Eating Facilities	Picnic facilities
Restroom Facilities	Yes
Handicapped Access	No
Additional Information	Free wine tastings

Pugliese Vineyards

THIS SMALL VINEYARD offers its visitors free wine-tasting experiences. During the season, demonstrations of wine pressing and a tour of the bottling facility are offered. The vineyards grow three specific grapes to produce a Chardonnay, a Cabernet Sauvignon and a Merlot.

Address/Telephone	Route 25A
	Cutchogue, NY 11935
	734-4057
When to Visit	Daily
	11:00 a.m. to 5:00 p.m.
Charges/Fees	None
Suggested Grades	K–Adult
Guided Tour	Yes, by appointment
Maximum Group	By arrangement
Group Notice	2 weeks
Eating Facilities	None
Restroom Facilities	Yes
Handicapped Access	Yes

Village Green Complex
(Cutchogue-New Suffolk Historical Council)

THE VILLAGE GREEN Complex, typifying the way of life for over 300 years on these and neighboring farmlands, features The Old House (1649), The Wickham Farm House (c. 1740), the Old School Museum (1840), and the Village Library (1862). The Old House is a registered National Historic Landmark. The School House was Cutchogue's first district school. A mid-19th century carriage house was recently added to the complex.

Address/Telephone	Village Green (Route 25) Cutchogue, NY 11935 734-7122
When to Visit	Saturday and Sunday—June and September Saturday to Monday—July and August 2:00 p.m. to 5:00 p.m. Groups (May 1 to October 31) by appointment
Charges/Fees	Adults—$1.50; children—$.50
Suggested Grades	3–Adult
Guided Tour	Yes, 1 hour
Maximum Group	By arrangement
Group Notice	2 weeks
Eating Facilities	Picnic facilities
Restroom Facilities	Yes
Handicapped Access	No
Additional Information	Admission covers visit to all buildings.

Willow Pet Hotel

THE WILLOW PET Hotel is the largest, most modern pet-boarding facility on the East Coast. Both registered and inspected by the Department of Agriculture, this facility is also one of the largest pet-grooming centers in the United States. This same facility operates a unique pet-transportation service, shipping both dogs and cats for relocated owners all over the world. Students will observe grooming operations through a glass window as some 40 to 70 animals are groomed each day. A tour through the cattery and dog-boarding areas will also take place.

Address/Telephone	1926 Deer Park Avenue
	Deer Park, NY 11729
	667-8924
When to Visit	Monday, Tuesday, Thursday, Friday and Saturday
	11:00 a.m. to 3:00 p.m.
Charges/Fees	None
Suggested Grades	3–9
Guided Tour	Yes, 15 to 30 minutes
Maximum Group	35, with 1 adult per group of 10
Group Notice	2 weeks
Eating Facilities	None
Restroom Facilities	Yes
Handicapped Access	No
Additional Information	Children should not touch the cages.

Adventureland
(Long Island's Amusement Park)

AS AN AMUSEMENT park, Adventureland provides some of the latest rides and special attractions found in theme parks around the nation. In terms of video and entertaining games, it has been described as a veritable warehouse of games. As a restaurant and eating establishment, Adventureland remains a legend on Long Island for its great hot dogs, deli sandwiches and pizza.

Address/Telephone	2245 Route 110
	East Farmingdale, NY 11735
	694-6868

When to Visit	Park Season—April to October
	Restaurant and Game Room—All year
Charges/Fees	Call for information and group rates
Suggested Grades	Pre-K–Adult
Guided Tour	None
Maximum Group	Unlimited
Group Notice	None
Eating Facilities	Yes
Restroom Facilities	Yes
Handicapped Access	Yes

The Boat Shop
(East Hampton Historical Society)

LOCATED ON THREE Mile Harbor, this educational facility is housed in a 19th-century converted barn on a commercial dock. Programming poossibilities include marine ecology, lofting, boat building, beachwalks and on-water programs in small vessels (sail and row).

Address/Telephone	*42 Gann Road
	East Hampton, NY 11937
	324-6850
When to Visit	By appointment
Charges/Fees	By arrangement
Suggested Grades	Pre-K–Adult
Guided Tour	Yes
Maximum Group	40
Group Notice	1 week minimum
Eating Facilities	None
Restroom Facilities	Yes
Handicapped Access	Yes
Additional Information	*Mailing address: 101 Main Street, East Hampton, NY 11937

Clinton Academy
(East Hampton Historical Society)

CLINTON ACADEMY, THE first academy chartered in New York State, served as a college preparatory school from 1784 to 1881 and later as a community center. It is now a museum that presents major interpretive exhibits from the East Hampton Historical Society's collections. There is also a collection of textiles, tools and equipment relating to local and regional history. Guided tours and classes are available.

Address/Telephone	151 Main Street East Hampton, NY 11937 324-1850
When to Visit	Saturday and Sunday—June Daily—July 4 to Labor Day 1:00 p.m. to 2:00 p.m. Groups call for appointment during summer and winter months
Charges/Fees	Public: Adults—$2.00; children—$1.00; seniors—$1.50 Schools: call for arrangements
Suggested Grades	Pre-K–Adult
Guided Tour	Gallery talks
Maximum Group	40, with adequate supervision
Group Notice	1 week
Eating Facilities	None
Restroom Facilities	Yes
Handicapped Access	No
Additional Information	Call for information on a variety of school programs. Tour begins at Mulford Farm.

Guild Hall Museum

GUILD HALL IS an art museum with a permanent collection of paintings, sculpture and works on paper by artists associated with the region, and is affiliated with the John Drew Theater (see separate entry). The schedule of contemporary art exhibitions and performing arts presentations continues year-round and a variety of educational programs are offered. Two major theater productions are launched each summer.

Address/Telephone	158 Main Street East Hampton, NY 11937 324-0806
When to Visit	Fall to Spring: Wednesday to Saturday—11:00 a.m. to 5:00 p.m. Sunday—Noon to 5:00 p.m. Summer: Daily—11:00 a.m. to 5:00 p.m.
Charges/Fees	Members—free; non-members—$2.00
Suggested Grades	K–Adult
Guided Tour	Yes, by arrangement
Maximum Group	60 (30 for guided tour)
Group Notice	2 weeks
Eating Facilities	None
Restroom Facilities	Yes
Handicapped Access	Yes
Additional Information	Write or call for calendar of events or summer theater brochure

Home Sweet Home Museum

THIS 17TH-CENTURY SALTBOX farmhouse was the childhood home of John Howard Payne, author of over 70 plays and the American copyright laws, champion of the rights of Native Americans and author of the poem "Home Sweet Home." The house is filled with furnishings from three centuries of East Hampton's history. The 1804 Pantigo Windmill, a fine example of early wooden technology, is located on the property.

Address/Telephone	14 James Lane East Hampton, NY 11937 324-0713
When to Visit	Monday to Saturday—10:00 a.m. to 4:00 p.m. Sunday—2:00 p.m. to 4:00 p.m.
Charges/Fees	Adults—$2.00; children—$1.00
Suggested Grades	4–Adult
Guided Tour	Yes, tour of house, grounds and windmill for school groups
Maximum Group	By arrangement
Group Notice	1 week
Eating Facilities	None
Restroom Facilities	None
Handicapped Access	No
Additional Information	Gift shop on premises

John Drew Theater of Guild Hall

THE JOHN DREW Theater, affiliated with Guild Hall, is a 400-seat auditorium in which musical and dramatic productions, lectures, films, dance recitals and concerts are held. Productions continue throughout the year and the theater offers a variety of educational programming to enhance appreciation and make the arts accessible to a broad audience.

Address/Telephone	158 Main Street East Hampton, NY 11937 324-0806
When to Visit	Programs scheduled all year. Call for latest times and dates.
Charges/Fees	Varies with program. Group discounts available.

Suggested Grades	K–Adult
Guided Tour	None
Maximum Group	60
Group Notice	2 weeks
Eating Facilities	None
Restroom Facilities	Yes
Handicapped Access	Yes
Additional Information	Infra-red hearing system for the hearing-impaired. Young People Theater Workshops and Summer Apprenticeship programs available.

Long Island Collection
(East Hampton Library)

THIS COLLECTION OF books, pamphlets, maps, newspapers, genealogies and government documents relating to the history and people of Long Island was originally donated by Morton Pannypacker. The Thomas Moran Biographical Art Collection and The Seversmith Collection (books and artifacts used in compiling his book on Colonial families of the region) are among the materials available, as well as special indexes to historical records.

Address/Telephone	159 Main Street East Hampton, NY 11937 324-0222
When to Visit	Monday to Wednesday, Friday and Saturday 1:00 p.m. to 4:30 p.m. Morning hours available by special appointment
Charges/Fees	None
Suggested Grades	4–Adult
Guided Tour	None
Maximum Group	15

Group Notice	1 month
Eating Facilities	Picnic facilities
Restroom Facilities	Yes
Handicapped Access	Ramp to main library for handicapped

Mulford Farm Complex
(East Hampton Historical Society)

THE MULFORD FARM is a unique complex of buildings that, until 1944, was used as a working farm. The farmhouse dates from 1680 and was maintained by one family for eight generations. It displays furniture and farm implements that help tell the history of a community and a family that lived and worked there.

Address/Telephone	10 James Lane East Hampton, NY 11937 324-6864
When to Visit	Saturday and Sunday—June Daily—July 4 to Labor Day 2:00 p.m. to 5:00 p.m. Groups: call for appointment during season and winter months.
Charges/Fees	Public: Adults—$2.00; children—$1.00; seniors—$1.50 Schools: call for arrangements
Suggested Grades	Pre-K–Adult
Guided Tour	Gallery talks
Maximum Group	40, with adequate supervision
Group Notice	1 week
Eating Facilities	None
Restroom Facilities	Yes
Handicapped Access	No
Additional Information	Call for information on a variety of school programs.

Old Hook Mill

TODAY EAST HAMPTON features the greatest concentration of windmills to be found anywhere in the United States. Old Hook Mill, built in 1806 by Nathaniel Dominy, is one of four mills located within the Village of East Hampton. The mill was refurbished and put into operating condition in 1939. Guided tours are given to all visitors.

Address/Telephone	*Montauk Highway East Hampton, NY 11937 324-0713
When to Visit	July and August Weekdays—10:00 a.m. to 4:00 p.m. Sunday—2:00 p.m. to 4:00 p.m.
Charges/Fees	Adults—$1.50; children—$1.00
Suggested Grades	4–Adult
Guided Tour	Yes, 15 minutes
Maximum Group	5
Group Notice	1 week
Eating Facilities	None
Restroom Facilities	None
Handicapped Access	No
Additional Information	*Mailing address: 14 James Lane, East Hampton, NY 11937

Osborn–Jackson House
(East Hampton Historical Society)

THE OSBORN-JACKSON HOUSE, dating from c. 1740, is one of the few remaining 18th-century houses in place on Main Street. Within the house are several 18th- and 19th-century period rooms that utilize decorative art pieces from the Society's collection. Seasonal exhibitions are occasionally on display as well. The house also serves as the Society's administrative offices.

Address/Telephone	101 Main Street East Hampton, NY 11937 324-6850
When to Visit	Temporarily closed as a museum, the facility presently serves as East Hampton Historical Society Headquarters. Call for reopening date.
Charges/Fees	Call for new fee schedule
Suggested Grades	K–Adult
Guided Tour	Gallery talks
Maximum Group	40, with adequate supervision
Group Notice	1 week
Eating Facilities	None
Restroom Facilities	Yes
Handicapped Access	No

Pollock Krasner House and Study Center

THIS HOUSE IS the former home and studio of the Abstract Expressionist painters Jackson Pollock and Lee Krasner, his wife. The Center's purposes are to preserve and interpret the site, which is highlighted by the paint-spattered floor on which Pollock created many of his masterpieces; and to provide facilities for research on 20th-century American art, with special emphasis on the artists' community of eastern Long Island. In addition to guided tours of the site, the program includes art exhibitions, lectures and special events during the summer season.

Address/Telephone	830 Fireplace Road East Hampton, NY 11937 324-4929
When to Visit	Open for guided tours by appointment Thursday, Friday and Saturday May to October 11:00 a.m. to 4:00 p.m. Study Center research collections open by appointment year-round.

Charges/Fees	$5.00 (lecture and special event tickets vary in price)
Suggested Grades	Pre-K–Adult
Guided Tour	By appointment, 45 minutes to 1 hour
Maximum Group	40
Group Notice	Individuals and small groups—1 week Bus tours and other large groups—1 month
Eating Facilities	None
Restroom Facilities	Yes
Handicapped Access	No

Town House Museum
(East Hampton Historical Society)

THIS FACILITY SERVED as the first town-meeting hall and schoolhouse. Originally located on the north end common, it was moved to three other locations before its final site next to Clinton Academy. The Town House was opened in summer 1989, providing visitors with an interactive East Hampton history "class" circa 1860, presented by a costumed interpreter.

Address/Telephone	149 Main Street East Hampton, NY 11937 324-6850
When to Visit	Saturday and Sunday—June Monday to Sunday—July 4 to Labor Day 1:00 p.m. to 2:00 p.m. Groups call for appointment during summer and winter months
Charges/Fees	Public: Adults—$2.00; children—$1.00; seniors—$1.50 Schools: Call for arrangements
Suggested Grades	Pre-K–Adult
Guided Tour	Yes, 1 hour
Maximum Group	40, with adequate supervision

Group Notice	1 week
Eating Facilities	None
Restroom Facilities	None
Handicapped Access	No
Additional Information	Call for information on a variety of school programs.

Bayway Arts Center

THE BAYWAY ARTS Center offers adult theater and children's shows. Whether it be *The Miracle Worker, Holiday for Toys,* a Broadway musical comedy or a mystery, Bayway caters to a broad audience. Holiday and seasonal shows are also produced. Evening performances on weekends and daytime shows for adults, older school groups and senior citizens are also offered.

Address/Telephone	265 East Main Street East Islip, NY 11730 581-2700
When to Visit	Friday and Saturday—8:30 p.m. Sunday—3:00 p.m. and 7:00 p.m. School and youth groups: Monday to Thursday— call for arrangements
Charges/Fees	Call for schedule
Suggested Grades	K–Adult, depending on program
Guided Tour	None
Maximum Group	250
Group Notice	General public—1 week Groups over 10—2 to 3 weeks
Eating Facilities	Yes, restaurant on premises
Restroom Facilities	Yes
Handicapped Access	No
Additional Information	Call for up-to-date information on programs and fees.

Long Island Greenbelt Trail

T HE LONG ISLAND Greenbelt Trail extends some 34 miles from the Great South Bay to Long Island Sound. Hikers may walk all or part of the trail, beginning at the Bay at Heckscher State Park or the Sound at Sunken Meadow State Park. The trail follows the Connetquot and Nissequogue River valleys through pine barrens and wetlands, over the moraines and through deciduous forests. Almost every plant and form of wildlife indigenous to Long Island can be found along the trail. The Long Island Greenbelt Trail Conference operates a number of other trails as well. Please write to the Central Islip address for further information.

Address/Telephone	*Heckscher State Park East Islip, NY 11730 Southern Terminus—581-1005 *Sunken Meadow State Park Kings Park, NY 11754 Northern Terminus—265-1054
When to Visit	Daily—dawn to dusk
Charges/Fees	Parking fee at State parks in summer
Suggested Grades	K–Adult
Guided Tour	See below
Maximum Group	By arrangement
Group Notice	Be sure to call for permission at least one day in advance
Eating Facilities	Picknicking, snack bars at terminus parks
Restroom Facilities	At State parks
Handicapped Access	No
Additional Information	Send for highly recommended map and instructions and tour information—$1.00 postage and handling. Map and instructions free at State parks. *Mailing address: Long Island Greenbelt Trail Conference, Inc., 23 Deer Path Road, Central Islip, NY 11722-3404

South Shore Nature Center
(Town of Islip)

THIS NATURE CENTER represents one of the few areas left on Long Island where an ecological balance between uplands, freshwater swamp and salt marsh has been preserved. It is situated on 200 acres. Visitors can walk its 2½ miles of nature trails with the aid of a guidebook or take one of the many special-subject guided walks offered at the center, where there is also a small natural history museum. There is also an instructional program available.

Address/Telephone	*Bayview Avenue East Islip, NY 11730 224-5436
When to Visit	Daily—April to October Monday to Friday—November to March 9:00 a.m. to 5:00 p.m.
Charges/Fees	Call for schedule of program and visitor fees
Suggested Grades	Pre-K–Adult
Guided Tour	By arrangement
Maximum Group	30, with adequate supervision
Group Notice	2 weeks
Eating Facilities	Picnic facilities
Restroom Facilities	Yes
Handicapped Access	No
Additional Information	*Mailing address: South Shore Nature Center, 50 Irish Lane, East Islip, NY 11730

Skydive Long Island

THIS SCHOOL AND training center represents Long Island's only student jump center. Skydiver's motto is "Train in the morning, jump in the afternoon." Beginners start with static line jumps and advance up to free-fall and tandem jumps. All instructors are U.S.P.A licensed. All jumpers are critiqued and First Jump Certificates are awarded.

Address/Telephone	Bart Spadaro's Airport 91 Montauk Highway East East Moriches, NY 11940 878-JUMP (878-5867)
When to Visit	April to November Wednesday to Friday—10:00 a.m. to sunset Saturday and Sunday—8:00 a.m. to sunset
Charges/Fees	$195.00—course, equipment and first jump $65.00—post-training jumps Call for group rates
Suggested Grades	Adults (18 and over)
Guided Tour	Training program
Maximum Group	30
Group Notice	2 weeks
Eating Facilities	Yes, nearby
Restroom Facilities	Yes
Handicapped Access	No
Additional Information	Jumpers must be under 225 pounds

Muttontown Preserve*

THIS PRESERVE, WHICH consists totally of over 500 acres, is a "living museum" set aside and protected in order to preserve nature as it once was. Both marked and unmarked trails are found throughout the preserve. Topographical features typical of the north shore, such as glacially formed rolling hills, are in evidence, along with kettle hole ponds, meadow and woodland. Equestrian trails for residents with horses are available throughout the entire property.

Address/Telephone	Muttontown Lane East Norwich, NY 11732 922-3123
When to Visit	Daily Groups—Monday to Friday 9:30 a.m. to 4:30 p.m.
Charges/Fees	Public—Free $20.00 per class/program

*Please note: East Norwich and Muttontown Preserve are located in Nassau County. See back of title page.

Suggested Grades	K–Adult
Guided Tour	Yes, 2 hours
Maximum Group	90
Group Notice	2 weeks
Eating Facilities	None
Restroom Facilities	Yes
Handicapped Access	Yes
Additional Information	Absolutely no collecting of plants or animals. Stay on trails. Operated by Nassau County Department of Recreation and Parks.

Swan River Schoolhouse Museum

THE SWAN RIVER Schoolhouse, built in 1858, was last used as a school in 1936. Now a museum, this former one-room schoolhouse shows typical school furniture, the original schoolhouse bell and books used by the students who attended this school.

Address/Telephone	Roe Avenue East Patchogue, NY 11772 475-1700
When to Visit	Daily (Usually closed Wednesday) June 15 to October 30 1:00 p.m. to 5:00 p.m. Groups by appointment
Charges/Fees	None
Suggested Grades	K–8
Guided Tour	Yes, about 15 minutes
Maximum Group	30
Group Notice	1 week
Eating Facilities	None
Restroom Facilities	None
Handicapped Access	No

Sherwood-Jayne House
(Society for the Preservation of Long Island Antiquities)

THIS SALTBOX HOUSE is filled with a varied collection of antiques and furnishings, pewter, textiles and paintings. Hand-painted wall frescoes are located in the east parlor and east bedroom and are discussed in major books on early American wall decoration.

Address/Telephone	Old Post Road
	East Setauket, NY 11733
	941-9444 Call: Society for the Preservation of Long Island Antiquities
When to Visit	By appointment
Charges/Fees	Adults—$1.50; children and seniors—$1.00
	Call for school discovery brochure and fees
Suggested Grades	2–Adult
Guided Tour	Yes, 45 minutes
Maximum Group	By arrangement
Group Notice	2 weeks
Eating Facilities	None
Restroom Facilities	None
Handicapped Access	No
Additional Information	Brochure available. Annual Shearing Festival held on grounds mid-May.

Broadhollow Children's Theater

THE STAGE LIGHTS up with shows for children most Saturday afternoons. Past and current productions include such shows as *The Diary of Anne Frank* and *Hansel and Gretel* as well as some that are appropriate for various holiday seasons. The theater offers evening performances on weekends and daytime shows for adults, older school groups and senior citizens.

Address/Telephone	229 Route 110 Farmingdale, NY 11735 752-1400

When to Visit	Children's shows: Saturday—1:00 p.m.
	Public: Friday—8:30 p.m.; Saturday—7:00 p.m. and
	   9:30 p.m.; Sunday—3:00 p.m. and 7:00 p.m.
	School and youth groups: Monday to Thursday—
	   call for appointments

Charges/Fees	Call for schedule
Suggested Grades	K–Adult, depending on program
Guided Tour	None
Maximum Group	175
Group Notice	General public—1 week. Groups over 10—2 to 3 weeks.
Eating Facilities	None
Restroom Facilities	Yes
Handicapped Access	No
Additional Information	Call for up-to-date information on programs and fees.

Republic Airport

REPUBLIC AIRPORT, EAST Farmingdale, provides educational and fun tours for children, adults and organizations. The tour consists of a visit to the Control Tower, the Crash/Fire/Rescue Operations and an aircraft hangar. At the Control Tower visitors are able to observe the FAA air traffic controllers conducting conversations with pilots and other air traffic control centers.

Address/Telephone	Route 110 Farmingdale, NY 11735 752-7707 Call: Fire Chief
When to Visit	Monday to Friday 10:00 a.m. to 11:00 p.m. Tours by appointment only
Charges/Fees	None

Suggested Grades	Pre-K–Adult
Guided Tour	Yes, 1½ hours
Maximum Group	20
Group Notice	2 weeks
Eating Facilities	Picnic facilities and vending machines available
Restroom Facilities	Yes
Handicapped Access	Yes
Additional Information	Trips to tower depend on operational considerations.

SUNY Printing Museum

THIS FACILITY CONSISTS of a working printing museum that features 19th- and early 20th-century printing equipment and hand-set type. The museum is set up like a complete job shop. All equipment is very well preserved and functional. Programs with hands-on involvement may be arranged.

Address/Telephone	SUNY College of Technology Hale Hall Farmingdale, NY 11735 420-2181
When to Visit	By appointment only during academic year Tuesday and Thursday 11:00 a.m. to noon Other days and times by special appointment
Charges/Fees	None
Suggested Grades	3–Adult
Guided Tour	By arrangement
Maximum Group	By arrangement
Group Notice	2 weeks
Eating Facilities	Yes
Restroom Facilities	Yes
Handicapped Access	Yes
Additional Information	A special tour of the college's high-tech printing shop can also be arranged as part of the visit.

Fire Island Coast Guard Station

T HIS COAST GUARD station serves as a base for search and rescue operations. A communications center, weather observation post and boats are part of the facility. The tour includes the main building and a close-up view of the boats. Visitors will have a chance to meet the personnel, see and hear the radios in operation and hear an explanation of the rescue process. Other areas of the station's responsibility include Law Enforcement and Marine Pollution Response.

Address/Telephone	*Robert Moses State Park Fire Island 661-9101 Call: Commanding Officer
When to Visit	Monday to Friday 9:00 a.m. to 11:00 a.m. and 1:00 p.m. to 4:00 p.m. Hours depend on current operations and availability of personnel. Groups tours only; we cannot accommodate groups under 10 persons, or individuals.
Charges/Fees	None
Suggested Grades	3–Adult
Guided Tour	Yes, 45 minutes to 1 hour
Maximum Group	30, with adequate supervision
Group Notice	1 month advance notice with confirmation is required.
Eating Facilities	None
Restroom Facilities	Yes
Handicapped Access	No
Additional Information	*Mailing address: Commanding Officer, USCG Station Fire Island, Babylon, NY 11702

Fire Island Lighthouse
(Fire Island National Seashore)

L OCATED AT THE western terminus of the National Seashore, the Lighthouse is accessible by automobile via Robert Moses Causeway. The Visitor Center is open to groups and the general public. The one-mile-long boardwalk trail provides access to both the Great South Bay and ocean beaches.

Address/Telephone	*Fire Island Lighthouse 661-4876
When to Visit	Open all year except Federal holidays 9:00 a.m. to 5:00 p.m. Visitor Center open April 19 to May 25 and September 7 to September 30: weekends and holidays—9:30 a.m. to 5:00 p.m. May 26 to September 6: Wednesday to Sunday— 9:30 a.m. to 5:00 p.m.
Charges/Fees	None
Suggested Grades	K–Adult
Guided Tour	By reservation only, 2 hours
Maximum Group	60
Group Notice	2 weeks
Eating Facilities	Nearby at Robert Moses State Park
Restroom Facilities	Yes
Handicapped Access	Yes
Additional Information	Danger: Strong surf and poison ivy. Ticks can cause health problems. *Mailing address: 120 Laurel Street, Patchogue, NY 11772

Smith Point
(Fire Island National Seashore)

S MITH POINT, THE eastern terminus of the National Seashore, is located at the southern end of William Floyd Parkway. A Visitor's Center with exhibits is on location. A trail ⅘ of a mile in length throughout the Point highlights the natural and cultural history of the area. There are parking and picnicking facilities adjacent to the Seashore at Smith Point County Park.

Address/Telephone	*Fire Island National Seashore 281-3010

When to Visit	Seashore: Open all year—9:00 a.m. to 5:00 p.m. Visitor Center: April 15 to December 31—8:00 a.m. to 4:00 p.m.
Charges/Fees	Parking fee at County Park
Suggested Grades	K–Adult
Guided Tour	Orientation programs and Environmental Education Programs—call in advance
Maximum Group	60
Group Notice	2 weeks
Eating Facilities	None
Restroom Facilities	Yes
Handicapped Access	Yes
Additional Information	Danger: Strong surf and poison ivy. Ticks can cause health problems. No lifeguard on duty. Boardwalk, lavatory and first floor of Visitor Center accessible to handicapped. Park Ranger is available upon request to present interpretive programs to school groups at their school if they cannot make it to Fire Island National Seashore. *Mailing address: 120 Laurel Street, Patchogue, NY 11772

Watch Hill
(Fire Island National Seashore)

WATCH HILL IS located in the eastern portion of the National Seashore Park. It provides 200 boat slips and includes water and electrical hookups. There are also camping facilities available for tents (no charge). A feature of this area of the Seashore is the large saltwater marsh and special nature trails. Watch Hill is adjacent to the National Wilderness Area. This Wilderness Area is the only National Wilderness Area in New York State.

Address/Telephone	Watch Hill 597-6455
When to Visit	May to October 9:00 a.m. to 6:00 p.m. Visitor Center: Daily, June 28 to September 7— 10:00 a.m. to 5:30 p.m.

Watch Hill

Charges/Fees	None
Suggested Grades	K–Adult
Guided Tour	Yes, interpretive talks and walks by arrangement. Check schedule for special films or other programs.
Maximum Group	By arrangement
Group Notice	None
Eating Facilities	Picnic facilities. Snack bar and restaurant, call 597-6655 for information.
Restroom Facilities	Yes
Handicapped Access	Yes
Additional Information	Danger: strong surf and poison ivy. Ticks can cause health problems.
	Call for current ferry rates and schedule. Davis Park Ferry Company, 475-1665. Camping reservations: 597-6633.
	*Mailing address: 120 Laurel Street, Patchogue, NY 11772

The Big Duck

PERHAPS LONG ISLAND'S most famous landmark, the Big Duck is recognized by architects and historians as one of America's finest examples of "Roadside Architecture." It was donated to Suffolk County in 1987. Plans are to restore the Big Duck as part of a "Museum of Roadside Culture" now being considered for the Flanders area.

Address/Telephone	*Route 24 Flanders, NY 11901 854-4971
When to Visit	Dawn to dusk
Charges/Fees	None
Suggested Grades	Pre-K–Adult
Guided Tour	None
Maximum Group	30
Group Notice	None
Eating Facilities	Picnic facilities nearby at Sears Bellows County Park
Restroom Facilities	Nearby at Sears Bellows County Park
Handicapped Access	Yes
Additional Information	No visit to Long Island is complete without a photograph of the Big Duck. Exterior viewing only. *Mailing address: Lance Mallano, c/o Suffolk County Parks, P.O. Box 144, W. Sayville, NY 11796

Bayard Cutting Arboretum

LOCATED ON 690 acres, this oasis of beauty and quiet contains numerous trees, shrubs and flower varieties. Many varieties of aquatic and land birds may be seen. There are several self-guided walks through the Arboretum. Located in the former Cutting residence is a natural history museum featuring an extensive collection of mounted birds. Concerts, meetings, classes and exhibits are presented at the Arboretum.

Address/Telephone	*466 Montauk Highway Great River, NY 11739 581-1002
When to Visit	May to October—10:00 a.m. to 5:30 p.m. November to April—10:00 a.m. to 4:30 p.m.
Charges/Fees	Vehicle fee: $3.00 Bus: Nonprofit—$10.00; others—$30.00 Call 669-1000 for up-to-date pricing structure.
Suggested Grades	K–Adult
Guided Tour	Yes, by special arrangement
Maximum Group	50 (groups over 50 and buses need permit)
Group Notice	2 weeks
Eating Facilities	Yes, May to October
Restroom Facilities	Yes
Handicapped Access	Yes
Additional Information	Every group leader must report to the director's office in the administration building. No food may be brought into the Arboretum from the outside. Museum is closed November to April. *Mailing address: P.O. Box 466, Oakdale, NY 11769

Greenlawn–Centerport Historical Association Museum

HOUSED IN THE Harborfields Public Library, this museum offers a growing collection of photographs, documents, genealogical information, objects and oral and written histories relating to Greenlawn and Centerport. Changing exhibits reflect the histories of the two communities and the lifestyles of the local people. There are demonstrations and educational programs offered by the museum.

Address/Telephone	31 Broadway Greenlawn, NY 11746 754-1180 or 754-4694
When to Visit	Wednesday and Thursday 1:00 p.m. to 4:00 p.m. Groups call for appointment
Charges/Fees	None
Suggested Grades	4–Adult
Guided Tour	Yes, call for further information
Maximum Group	25
Group Notice	3 weeks
Eating Facilities	None
Restroom Facilities	Yes
Handicapped Access	Yes
Additional Information	Located in Harborfields Public Library building. Programs may be designed according to group needs and interests.

Stirling Historical Society and Museum

THIS 1831 HOMESTEAD serves both as a village museum and the Stirling Historical Society's headquarters. Located in Monsell Park, the Museum is a good place to acquaint oneself with the history of Greenport and then casually walk the quaint streets of the village, which are filled with many early homes. This old fishing, shipbuilding and whaling village saw many famous guests, such as John Quincy Adams, General Winfield Scott and Admiral George Dewey during its earlier days.

Address/Telephone	*Main Street Greenport, NY 11944 477-0099
When to Visit	Wednesday, Saturday and Sunday July to September 1:00 p.m. to 4:00 p.m.

Charges/Fees	$.50
Suggested Grades	4–Adult
Guided Tour	Yes, by arrangement
Maximum Group	30
Group Notice	1 week
Eating Facilities	None
Restroom Facilities	None
Handicapped Access	No
Additional Information	*Mailing address: P.O. Box 590, Greenport, NY 11944

Shinnecock Coast Guard Station

THIS COAST GUARD station serves as a base for search and rescue operations. A communications center, weather observation post and boats are part of the facility. The tour includes the main building and a close-up view of the boats. Visitors will have a chance to meet the personnel, see and hear the radios in operation and hear an explanation of the rescue process. Other areas of the station's responsibility include maintenance of Aids to Navigation, Law Enforcement and Marine Pollution Investigation.

Address/Telephone	100 Foster Avenue Hampton Bays, NY 11946 728-0078 Call: Commanding Officer
When to Visit	Monday to Saturday 9:00 a.m. to 11:00 a.m. and 1:00 p.m. to 4:00 p.m.
Charges/Fees	None
Suggested Grades	3–12
Guided Tour	Yes, 30 minutes
Maximum Group	30, with 1 adult per group of 8
Group Notice	1 month
Eating Facilities	None
Restroom Facilities	Yes
Handicapped Access	No

Brookhaven Service Center
(Internal Revenue Service)

A T THE BROOKHAVEN Service Center visitors will see where the processing of up to 18 million business and individual tax returns from the New York metropolitan area are processed yearly. Located on a 67-acre tract of land, the Center consists of a five-building complex that contains over a half-million square feet of space. This modern facility contains office and workspace for up to 5,000 employees during peak periods as well as a computer center housing some very sophisticated computers and processing equipment.

Address/Telephone	1040 Waverly Avenue
	Holtsville, NY 11799
	654-6030 Call: Public Affairs
When to Visit	Monday to Friday
	May to October
	9:00 a.m. to 3:30 p.m.
Charges/Fees	None
Suggested Grades	12th grade and college business majors only
Guided Tour	Yes, 1 to 2 hours in length
Maximum Group	Unlimited
Group Notice	2 weeks
Eating Facilities	Call for special arrangements
Restroom Facilities	Yes
Handicapped Access	Yes

Holtsville Park and Zoo
(Town of Brookhaven)

O NCE A GARBAGE dump, this site is now a thriving recreational park. Visitors may walk on hills made from garbage that now have trees and wildflowers growing on them, or may visit a barnyard and native North American zoo, home to many permanently injured animals. One can get a close-up look at how leaves are recycled into compost, which is then used to enrich the soil. There is a jogging and exercise trail, swimming pools, picnic area and playground available.

Address/Telephone	249 Buckley Road Holtsville, NY 11742 758-9664
When to Visit	Park: Daily—9:00 a.m. to dusk Zoo: Daily—9:00 a.m. to 4:00 p.m. (extended hours in summer)
Charges/Fees	None (except for fee at pools)
Suggested Grades	1–Adult
Guided Tour	Yes, 1½ hour tour, including talk on problems of resource recovery, endangered species and wild-life habitats
Maximum Group	30
Group Notice	2 weeks to 6 months, depending on season
Eating Facilities	Picnic facilities all year and snack bar in picnic area during July and August only
Restroom Facilities	Yes
Handicapped Access	Yes
Additional Information	Wear walking shoes and dress appropriately for outdoor tour.

Conklin House
(Huntington Historical Society)

THE CONKLIN HOUSE, built c. 1750, is a farmhouse that reflects the changes that were often made in homes as they were adapted to meet the family's changing needs. Inhabited until 1911, it is maintained by the Huntington Historical Society as a museum of local history and the decorative arts. There is a guided tour.

Address/Telephone	*2 High Street Huntington, NY 11743 427-7045

When to Visit	Tuesday to Friday and Sunday
	1:00 p.m. to 4:00 p.m.
	Groups: Tuesday to Thursday (by appointment)
	9:00 a.m. to noon
Charges/Fees	Adults—$2.00; children—$.75; seniors—$1.00
Suggested Grades	1–Adult
Guided Tour	Yes, 90 minutes for school groups
Maximum Group	30, with 2 adults
Group Notice	2 weeks
Eating Facilities	None
Restroom Facilities	Emergency only
Handicapped Access	No
Additional Information	Special 90-minute program with demonstrations and hands-on crafts available for school groups. Preview slide program with activity pack provided for classroom use prior to visit.
	*Mailing address: 209 Main Street, Huntington, NY 11743

Heckscher Museum

ON DISPLAY ARE paintings, sculptures and prints from the Heckscher Museum's permanent collection of over 800 objects ranging from 15th-century European masterpieces to the work of contemporary American artists. The Museum presents an ambitious schedule of temporary exhibitions on an every-six-to-eight-week basis. These exhibits vary from the historical to the contemporary and from showcasing international artists to explorations of the work of Long Island artists.

Address/Telephone	Route 25A and Prime Avenue
	Huntington, NY 11743
	351-3250
When to Visit	Tuesday to Friday—10:00 a.m. to 5:00 p.m.
	Saturday and Sunday—1:00 p.m. to 5:00 p.m.
Charges/Fees	$2.00 (suggested); children—$1.00
Suggested Grades	All ages

Guided Tour	Yes, 1 hour. Discovery Program for school groups: grades N–K—1½ hours; grades 1–12—2 hours.
Maximum Group	40, with adequate supervision
Group Notice	3 weeks
Eating Facilities	Picnic facilities
Restroom Facilities	Yes
Handicapped Access	No
Additional Information	Arrangements may be made for Discovery Program, hands-on art workshops for school groups, Pre-K through adult. For reservations and information on exhibit-related public programs call 351-3250. Sunday Gallery Talks (2:30 p.m.)—no reservations required.

The Huntington Arsenal
(Town of Huntington)

THIS FULLY RESTORED building was used to store arms and ammunition during the Colonial and Revolutionary periods. Members of the Huntington Militia are present in Colonial dress, demonstrating household crafts, candle-dipping and Revolutionary-era military equipment.

Address/Telephone	425 Park Avenue Huntington, NY 11743 351-3244
When to Visit	Sunday 1:00 p.m. to 4:00 p.m. Call if special arrangements are needed for groups.
Charges/Fees	None
Suggested Grades	K–Adult
Guided Tour	Yes, 30 minutes
Maximum Group	20
Group Notice	1 month
Eating Facilities	None
Restroom Facilities	None
Handicapped Access	No

Huntington Sewing and Trade School
(Huntington Historical Society)

THE HUNTINGTON SEWING and Trade School was built in 1905 and is a recent acquisition of the Huntington Historical Society. It houses the Society's administrative offices and the library, which contains books, manuscripts, photographs and genealogies on Huntington and Long Island.

Address/Telephone	209 Main Street Huntington, NY 11743 427-7045
When to Visit	Tuesday to Friday—1:00 p.m. to 4:00 p.m. Second Saturday of each month—10:00 p.m. to 4:00 p.m., by appointment Other times by special appointment
Charges/Fees	$2.00 per person per day for use of the library
Suggested Grades	4–Adult
Guided Tour	None
Maximum Group	None
Group Notice	None
Eating Facilities	None
Restroom Facilities	Yes
Handicapped Access	No

Kissam House
(Huntington Historical Society)

THE KISSAM HOUSE was built in 1795 and is a museum of period rooms in the Colonial, Empire and Federal styles; Long Island paintings; and an outstanding collection of antique costumes. Built by Timothy Jarvis, a housewright, it boasts many fine architectural details. Adjacent to the barn is the Museum Shop, an emporium of gifts, antiques and craft items.

Address/Telephone	*434 Park Avenue Huntington, NY 11743 427-7045
When to Visit	1:00 p.m. to 4:00 p.m. (by appointment) Groups: Tuesday to Thursday 9:00 a.m. to noon (by appointment)
Charges/Fees	Adults—$2.00; children—$.75; seniors—$1.00
Suggested Grades	1–Adult
Guided Tour	Yes, 90 minutes for school groups
Maximum Group	30, with 2 adults
Group Notice	2 weeks
Eating Facilities	None
Restroom Facilities	Emergency only
Handicapped Access	No
Additional Information	Special 90-minute program with demonstrations and hands-on crafts available for school groups. Preview slide program with activity pack provided for classroom use prior to visit. *Mailing address: 209 Main Street, Huntington, NY 11743

Little Jennie
(Maritime Center on Long Island)

BUILT IN 1884 and completely restored by the Maritime Center, the 86-foot sailing vessel *Little Jennie* is available to organizations for programs in environmental and ecological awareness. Fully certified by the U.S. Coast Guard, this sailing vessel is equipped to carry up to 30 passengers on educational excursions on Long Island Sound. The Maritime Center is presently in the process of restoring a motorized passenger vessel for expanded programs and tours.

Address/Telephone	*New York Avenue Town of Huntington Dock Huntington, NY 11743 385-7743

When to Visit	Monday to Saturday April 1 to November 1
Charges/Fees	Call for information
Suggested Grades	4–Adult
Guided Tour	Marine Biology, Coastal Ecology and Environmental programs designed according to group needs
Maximum Group	30
Group Notice	Make arrangements well in advance
Eating Facilities	"Brown bag"
Restroom Facilities	Yes
Handicapped Access	No
Additional Information	Full-day and half-day programs available. Special programs and activities by arrangement. *Mailing address: Maritime Center on Long Island, P.O. Box 991, Huntington, NY 11743

Soldiers and Sailors Memorial Building
(Town of Huntington)

B UILT IN 1892, this structure was planned both as a memorial for those who gave their lives in the Civil War and as a home for the Huntington Library Association. Today it houses the office of the Huntington Town historian and stores old town records and memorabilia. This building is now listed on the National Register of Historic Places.

Address/Telephone	228 Main Street (Route 25A) Huntington, NY 11743 351-3244
When to Visit	Monday to Friday 8:30 a.m. to 4:30 p.m.
Charges/Fees	None
Suggested Grades	4–Adult
Guided Tour	30-minute talk

Maximum Group	40
Group Notice	1 week
Eating Facilities	None
Restroom Facilities	Emergency only
Handicapped Access	Yes

Walt Whitman Birthplace State Historic Site

THIS SHINGLED FARMHOUSE, Walt Whitman's birthplace and home for four of his childhood years, was built in 1819 by the poet's father and features many unusual architectural aspects. On display are authentic pieces of 19th-century furniture as well as the schoolmaster's desk and secretary used by him. The second floor contains a library of several hundred volumes, monographs and catalogs, and an exhibit of photos, letters, books and other memorabilia through which one may browse or read and immerse oneself in the world of the distinguished poet.

Address/Telephone	246 Old Walt Whitman Road Huntington Station, NY 11746 427-5240
When to Visit	Wednesday to Friday—1:00 p.m. to 4:00 p.m. Saturday and Sunday—10:00 a.m. to 4:00 p.m. Closed holidays.
Charges/Fees	None
Suggested Grades	2–Adult
Guided Tour	Yes
Maximum Group	48, with adequate supervision
Group Notice	2 weeks
Eating Facilities	Picnic facilities and restaurants
Restroom Facilities	Yes
Handicapped Access	No
Additional Information	Video program—18 minutes. Museum shop on premises.

Jamesport Vineyards

JAMESPORT VINEYARDS PRODUCES eight varieties of grapes and eight varieties of wine on its 40-acre vineyard. Visitors are given the opportunity to visit the tasting room and speak with a representative of the winery, while sampling the vintages currently available for purchasing.

Address/Telephone	Main Road
	Jamesport, NY 11947
	722-5256 (winery)
	364-3633 (office)
When to Visit	May to December
	10:00 a.m. to 5:00 p.m.
	Call for schedule of times and events
Charges/Fees	None
Suggested Grades	K–Adult
Guided Tour	By request
Maximum Group	By arrangement
Group Notice	1 week
Eating Facilities	None
Restroom Facilities	Yes
Handicapped Access	Yes

BOCES Outdoor Environmental Education Program
(Sunken Meadow State Park)

THE PRESENT AREA of Sunken Meadow State Park owes its preservation to acquisition by New York State, which gradually purchased a number of parcels of land from private persons and the Town of Smithtown. The park is comprised of 1,266 acres, which include a rocky intertidal area, sandy beach, salt marsh, climax forest vegetation and a portion of the Harbor Hill Moraine that extends along Long Island's north shore. Learning Lab contains a variety of interesting displays concerning the natural history of Long Island. Aquaria contain numerous marine and freshwater species.

Address/Telephone	Sunken Meadow State Park
	Parking Field #5
	Kings Park, NY 11754
	269-4343
When to Visit	Monday to Friday
	8:30 p.m. to 5:00 p.m.
	Summer and weekend programs by special arrangement
	Environmental World Summer Program (July and August)—parents may call 360-0800
Charges/Fees	BOCES shared service aid available
Suggested Grades	Pre-K–Adult
Guided Tour	By request
Maximum Group	30
Group Notice	By April of previous school year
Eating Facilities	Indoor/outdoor—picnic or "brown bag"
Restroom Facilities	Yes
Handicapped Access	Yes
Additional Information	Write for literature

Canoe the Nissequogue River
(Bob's Canoe Rental, Inc.)

THIS CANOE TRIP usually begins at "The Bluffs" at Kings Park where the Nissequogue empties into Long Island Sound. Timing is very critical when paddling up or down the Nissequogue since it is an estuary. A rising tide gives one the advantage when paddling from the mouth to the headwaters. Likewise, a falling tide gives the advantage when paddling downstream toward the Sound. Paddling through the reeds and marshes up the winding Nissequogue brings one to Caleb Smith State Park and the original site of three mills, one of which is still standing. The trip may begin at either end of the Nissequogue depending on the tide.

Address/Telephone	"River Mouth" *Foot of Old Dock Road Kings Park, NY 11754 269-9761
	"Headwaters" *Paul T. Given Riverside Conservation Area Routes 25 and 25A (opposite the Bull) Smithtown, NY 269-9761
When to Visit	Daily
Charges/Fees	$30.00—1 canoe Call for group rates
Suggested Grades	K–Adult—adequate supervision mandatory
Guided Tour	Map of River provided
Maximum Group	144 (at 4 persons per canoe)
Group Notice	1 week
Eating Facilities	Picnic at appropriate sites along river Restaurant at mouth of river
Restroom Facilities	At Kings Park
Handicapped Access	No
Additional Information	Life jackets and paddles provided. Transportation back to car provided for one-way paddlers. Bob's Canoe Rental can also arrange trips on the Peconic and Carmans Rivers (call for information). *Mailing address: P.O. Box 529, Kings Park, NY 11754

Canoe the Nissequogue River
(Nissequogue River Canoe Rentals)

THIS CANOE TRIP begins at "The Bluffs" at Kings Park where the Nissequogue empties into Long Island Sound. Timing is very critical when paddling up or down the Nissequogue since it is an estuary. A rising tide gives one the advantage when paddling from the mouth to the headwaters. Likewise, a falling tide gives the advantage when paddling downstream toward the Sound. Paddling through the reeds and marshes up the winding Nissequogue brings one to Caleb Smith State Park and the original site of three mills, one of which is still standing. The trip may begin at either end of the Nissequogue depending on the tide.

Address/Telephone	"River Mouth" *Foot of Old Dock Road Kings Park, NY 11754 979-8244
	"Headwaters" *Paul T. Given Riverside Conservation Area Routes 25 and 25A (opposite the Bull) Smithtown, NY 979-8244
When to Visit	Daily
Charges/Fees	$30.00—1 canoe Call for group rates
Suggested Grades	K–Adult—adequate supervision mandatory
Guided Tour	Available
Maximum Group	160 (at 4 persons per canoe)
Group Notice	1 week
Eating Facilities	Picnic at appropriate sites along river Restaurant at mouth of river
Restroom Facilities	At Kings Park
Handicapped Access	No
Additional Information	Life jackets and paddles provided. Transportation back to car provided for one-way paddlers. *Mailing address: 112 Whittier Drive, Kings Park, NY 11754

Obadiah Smith House
(Smithtown Historical Society)

THIS HOUSE WAS constructed in the early 18th century with many 17th-century features. The dwelling's floor plan is similar to that of other houses built by the early descendants of Smithtown's original patentee. Of particular interest is the kitchen with its large fireplace and unusual construction. The house is backed up to a hill on its north side for protection from the winter winds. Bridges were built in order to gain access from the second floor to the hillside.

Address/Telephone	853 St. Johnland Road
	Kings Park, NY 11754
	265-6768
When to Visit	By appointment
Charges/Fees	Adults—$1.00; children—$.25
Suggested Grades	2–Adult
Guided Tour	Yes, 30 to 60 minutes in length
Maximum Group	25, with adequate supervision
Group Notice	2 weeks
Eating Facilities	None
Restroom Facilities	Yes
Handicapped Access	No
Additional Information	Programs and demonstrations by special arrangement

American Merchant Marine Museum*

THE COLLECTION AT this museum offers some 35 ship models, among them an 18-foot model of the famous passenger ship SS *Washington*. Also on display are rare antique navigational instruments, an unusual collection of coffee cups and the trophy for the fastest transatlantic crossing by a passenger liner. There is also a Maritime Hall of Fame, as well as maritime artworks and photographs.

Address/Telephone	Steamboat Road
	Kings Point, NY 11024
	466-9696
When to Visit	Saturday and Sunday
	1:00 p.m. to 5:00 p.m.
	Groups: Monday to Thursday, by appointment
Charges/Fees	None
Suggested Grades	3–Adult

*Please note: Kings Point and the American Merchant Marine Museum are located in Nassau County. See back of title page.

American Merchant Marine Museum

Guided Tour	Yes, for groups by arrangement
Maximum Group	30
Group Notice	2 weeks
Eating Facilities	Picnic facilities
Restroom Facilities	Yes
Handicapped Access	No

United States Merchant Marine Academy*

THIS ACADEMY WAS founded in 1943 to prepare young men and women as officers for the American merchant marine and for leadership positions in the maritime industry. Visitors will observe midshipmen training for various careers within the industry. Midshipmen also appear in full dress parade on selected Saturdays in the spring and fall. Points of interest on campus include the Mariners Chapel and the American Merchant Marine Museum.

Address/Telephone	Kings Point, NY 11024
	773-5387 Call: Office of External Affairs
When to Visit	Open all year except July and federal holidays
Charges/Fees	None
Suggested Grades	K–Adult
Guided Tour	Yes, 1 hour
Maximum Group	40
Group Notice	2 weeks
Eating Facilities	Picnic facilities
Restroom Facilities	Yes
Handicapped Access	No
Additional Information	Speakers available for high schools only

First Congressional Church of New Village

THIS CHURCH, WHICH now serves as a town museum, was built in 1817. The structure represents a typical old-fashioned country church. The shingled wood-frame building is a good example of period architecture and still includes some of the original windowpanes as well as some unique features.

Address/Telephone	Middle Country Road
	Lake Grove, NY 11755
	473-6221 Call: Mr. Overton

*Please note: Kings Point and the United States Merchant Marine Academy are located in Nassau County. See back of title page.

When to Visit	Daily
	1:00 p.m. to 5:00 p.m.
	Groups by appointment
Charges/Fees	None
Suggested Grades	K–Adult
Guided Tour	Yes, 15 minutes
Maximum Group	30
Group Notice	2 weeks
Eating Facilities	None
Restroom Facilities	None
Handicapped Access	No

Lake Ronkonkoma Historical Museum
(Lake Ronkonkoma Historical Society)

THIS MUSEUM, MAINTAINED by the Society, contains a collection of period postcards, maps, Long Island Indian artifacts and local family memorabilia from the Lake Ronkonkoma area. It offers the visitor a glimpse of the changing scenes around the lake from a small farming community to a haven for scores of people who enjoy boating, bathing and picnicking on its shores.

Address/Telephone	328 Hawkins Avenue
	Lake Ronkonkoma, NY 11779
	467-3152
When to Visit	Public: Monday and Saturday—March to December
	Monday—July 4 to Labor Day
	10:00 a.m. to noon
	Groups by appointment
Charges/Fees	Donation
Suggested Grades	Pre-K–Adult
Guided Tour	By arrangement, 1 hour
Maximum Group	25
Group Notice	2 weeks
Eating Facilities	None
Restroom Facilities	Yes
Handicapped Access	No

1901 Depot Restoration and Freighthouse

VISITORS WILL OBSERVE a complete restoration of a turn-of-the-century railroad depot and freighthouse. Inside the freighthouse is an exhibit depicting the types of trunks, barrels and specialized shipping crates used at the time, as well as the outfits and uniforms worn by railroad personnel. The story of "Mile-a-Minute" Murphy and exhibits of other railroad artifacts are on display.

Address/Telephone	South Broadway and South Third Street
	Lindenhurst, NY 11757
	226-1254
When to Visit	Monday to Friday
	July and August
	1:00 p.m. to 3:00 p.m.
Charges/Fees	None
Suggested Grades	K–Adult
Guided Tour	Yes, 45 minutes, by appointment
Maximum Group	30
Group Notice	2 weeks
Eating Facilities	None
Restroom Facilities	None
Handicapped Access	No

Old Village Hall Museum

THIS MUSEUM WAS the first village-owned seat of government, containing a courtroom, the village clerk's office and a police station. Today it contains displays of articles belonging to the first permanent settlers, mementos of the Wellwood family and an exhibit tracing the evolution of Neguntatogue into Lindenhurst.

Address/Telephone	215 S. Wellwood Avenue
	Lindenhurst, NY 11757
	957-4385 Call: Director

When to Visit	Wednesday, Friday, Saturday and first Sunday of each month—October to May Monday, Wednesday and Friday—June to September 2:00 p.m. to 4:00 p.m. Groups by appointment
Charges/Fees	None
Suggested Grades	4–Adult
Guided Tour	Yes, 45 to 60 minutes
Maximum Group	25, with 1 adult per group of 10
Group Notice	2 weeks
Eating Facilities	None
Restroom Facilities	None
Handicapped Access	Yes

Studio Theater

STUDIO THEATER CATERS to adult audiences during evening-only performances. Productions include traditional musicals, comedies and new works as well as esoteric and avant-garde productions. Murder mysteries with audience participation offer an exciting and challenging evening for audiences.

Address/Telephone	141 S. Wellwood Avenue Lindenhurst, NY 11757 226-1833
When to Visit	Wednesday—8:00 p.m.; Friday—8:30 p.m.; Saturday—8:00 p.m.; Sunday—3:00 p.m. and 7:00 p.m. Groups call for arrangements
Charges/Fees	Call for schedule
Suggested Grades	Adult
Guided Tour	None
Maximum Group	142

Group Notice	General public—1 week; groups over 10—2 to 3 weeks
Eating Facilities	None
Restroom Facilities	Yes
Handicapped Access	No
Additional Information	Call for up-to-date information on programs and fees.

Joseph Lloyd Manor House
(Society for the Preservation of Long Island Antiquities)

L LOYD MANOR, BUILT in 1766, is a handsome structure with fine interior woodwork by Connecticut craftsmen. Located in a spectacular setting overlooking Lloyd Harbor, the grounds contain a formal garden. The house is furnished to the 1793 inventory of John Lloyd II. Lloyd Manor was the home of Jupiter Hammon, a slave who became the first published black poet in America. Interpretive exhibits provide the history and documentation for the installation.

Address/Telephone	Lloyd Lane Lloyd Harbor, NY 11743 941-9444 Call: Society for the Preservation of Long Island Antiquities
When to Visit	Saturday and Sunday May to mid-October 1:00 p.m. to 5:00 p.m.
Charges/Fees	Adults—$1.50; children and seniors—$1.00 Call for School Discovery Brochure and fees
Suggested Grades	2–Adult
Guided Tour	Yes, approximately 30 minutes
Maximum Group	Call for arrangements
Group Notice	2 weeks
Eating Facilities	None
Restroom Facilities	Yes
Handicapped Access	No
Additional Information	Brochure available

Volunteers for Wildlife

V OLUNTEERS FOR WILDLIFE is a nonprofit wildlife rehabilitation and education organization, founded in 1982 to help provide rescue assistance, medical care and rehabilitation for injured and distressed wildlife on Long Island. The Volunteers for Wildlife Rehabilitation and Education Center at Caumsett State Park houses the treatment and care facility for injured and recovering wildlife. The organization provides workshops and internships to train those interested in wildlife rehabilitation. Additionally, Volunteers for Wildlife offers schools, scout groups, libraries and community organizations a selection of educational programs about Long Island wildlife.

Address/Telephone	*Caumsett State Park West Neck Road Lloyd Harbor, NY 11743 423-0982
When to Visit	By appointment
Charges/Fees	Programs at schools—$75.00 per program Programs at Caumsett Park Facility—$55.00 per program
Suggested Grades	Pre-K–Adult
Guided Tour	Call for schedule of program and tours
Maximum Group	30
Group Notice	1 month
Eating Facilities	"Brown bag"
Restroom Facilities	Yes
Handicapped Access	Yes
Additional Information	*Mailing address: Volunteers for Wildlife, Inc., 27 Lloyd Harbor Road, Huntington, NY 11743

Target Rock National Wildlife Refuge

T ARGET ROCK REFUGE is a national home for many types of wildlife. Rhododendron and azalea gardens make a spring visit an exceptional treat. A system of nature trails will provide excellent opportunities for bird watching, hiking and photography. Of special interest is the concentration of warblers during their May migration. There is access to beachfront on Huntington Bay for fishing.

Address/Telephone	Target Rock Road Lloyd Neck, NY 11743 271-2409 or 286-0485
When to Visit	Daily Sunrise to sunset

Charges/Fees	Car and occupants—$3.00; Walk-in and
	    bicyclists—$1.00
	Yearly passes available.
	Free lifetime passes for senior citizens and the
	    disabled are available.

Suggested Grades	K–Adult
Guided Tour	None
Maximum Group	50, with adequate supervision
Group Notice	2 weeks
Eating Facilities	None
Restroom Facilities	Yes
Handicapped Access	No
Additional Information	Limited parking. Poison ivy on trails. Wear appropriate footwear. Ticks can be dangerous.

The Animal Farm Petting Zoo

NOT A ZOO, but a farm, this is the perfect place to gently introduce children to the world of animals. Here they may see, feed and pet the animals including bunnies, cows, sheep and goats. As part of the farm one can see the largest selection of rare and exotic poultry on Long Island. Also on display are burros, monkeys, kangaroos, llamas and deer.

Address/Telephone	184A Wading River Road Manorville, NY 11949 878-1785

When to Visit	Daily mid-March to October 10:00 a.m. to 5:00 p.m.
Charges/Fees	Adults—$8.00; children and seniors—$6.00; children under 2—free Groups call for appointments and rates
Suggested Grades	Pre-K–Adult
Guided Tour	Yes, 2 to 3 hours
Maximum Group	500
Group Notice	1 week
Eating Facilities	Yes, snack bar and picnic facilities
Restroom Facilities	Yes
Handicapped Access	No
Additional Information	Entrance fee includes pony ride and two separate kiddy train rides. Tour includes animal show and puppet show. A playground is also located on the premises. Take L.I. Expressway exit 69, then south 3 miles on Wading River Road.

Long Island Game Farm Children's Zoo & Family Ride Park

THE LONG ISLAND Game Farm specializes in petting areas, including: Bambiland, where you wander among the deer and hand-feed them; the Nursery, where you can bottle feed the babies; and Old MacDonald's Farmyard. It also has exotic animals including zebra, camels, tigers, chimpanzee, ostrich, buffalo and more! It has an Antique Carousel, 1860s Iron Horse Train Ride, Playport, Swings, Castle Bound and Sky Slide. And it has daily Wild Bengal Tiger Shows and Animal Wonderland Shows.

Address/Telephone	Chapman Boulevard Manorville, NY 11949 878-6644 Call: Education Dept.

When to Visit	Daily mid-April to mid-October 10:00 a.m. to 6:00 p.m.
Charges/Fees	Adults—$11.95; children (2–11) and seniors—$8.95; children under 2—free Call for group rates
Suggested Grades	Pre-K–Adult
Guided Tour	None
Maximum Group	Unlimited, with adequate supervision
Group Notice	2 weeks, for catered picnics and birthday pavilion
Eating Facilities	Picnic facilities and refreshment stand
Restroom Facilities	Yes
Handicapped Access	Yes
Additional Information	Admission includes all rides, shows and attractions, except for Sky Slide.

William Floyd Estate
(Fire Island National Seashore)

TWO HUNDRED AND fifty years of history are preserved at the William Floyd Estate. Between 1718 and 1976, eight generations of Floyds managed the property and adapted it to their changing needs. The 25-room Old House, the 12 outbuildings, the graveyard and the 613 acres of forest, field and marsh illustrate the Floyd Family history in Mastic.

Address/Telephone	245 Park Drive Mastic Beach, NY 11951 4 blocks north of the eastern terminus of Neighborhood Road in Mastic Beach 399-2030
When to Visit	Open weekends only May to September

Charges/Fees	None
Suggested Grades	4–Adult
Guided Tour	As funding permits—please call 399-2030
Maximum Group	24, with adequate supervision
Group Notice	1 month—mandatory
Eating Facilities	Picnic tables provided
Restroom Facilities	Port-a-lavs
Handicapped Access	Yes
Additional Information	Site Operations are based on funding received each year. Please call site staff and inquire as to the status of school programs. Site staff does maintain a waiting list.

American Armoured Foundation, Inc.

AMERICAN ARMOURED FOUNDATION, Inc. is one of the largest tank and ordnance war memorial museums in the United States. A.A.F. is a "living" museum dedicated to honoring all veterans. The museum's specialty is to restore and preserve tanks and artillery. Presently on display are over 65 tanks and artillery pieces from the Spanish–American War through Operation Desert Storm. Also on hand: a large collection of tank uniforms and helmets, over 40 international military rifles and a weapons room that displays over 150 machine-gun-size weapons from around the world.

Address/Telephone	*Love Lane Mattituck, NY 11952 588-0033
When to Visit	Sunday 11:00 a.m. to 4:00 p.m.
Charges/Fees	Adults—$5.00; children (6–12) and seniors—$4.00; children under 5—free
Suggested Grades	K–Adult
Guided Tour	Yes, 1 to 2 hours (by appointment only)
Maximum Group	40
Group Notice	2 weeks (with deposit)

American Armoured Foundation

Eating Facilities	No
Restroom Facilities	Yes
Handicapped Access	Yes
Additional Information	Minimum group for a tour is 20 people. *Mailing address: 2383 Fifth Avenue, Ronkonkoma, NY 11779

Mattituck Historical Museum and Schoolhouse
(Mattituck Historical Society)

HOUSED IN A building constructed in 1800 and expanded in 1841, this museum is furnished with antiques of the period and displays of toys and rare musical instruments. Other exhibits include century-old clothing, guns, quilts, maps and arrowheads. There is also an 1864 schoolhouse, a milk house and barn on the site.

Address/Telephone	*Main Road (Route 25) Mattituck, NY 11952 298-5911
When to Visit	Public: Saturday and Sunday July 1 to Labor Day Schools and groups: by appointment Memorial Day to mid-October 2:00 p.m. to 4:00 p.m.
Charges/Fees	Adults—$2.00; children—$1.00
Suggested Grades	3–Adult
Guided Tour	Yes, 1 to 2 hours
Maximum Group	25, with adequate supervision
Group Notice	2 weeks
Eating Facilities	None
Restroom Facilities	Yes
Handicapped Access	No
Additional Information	Summer months feature special activities on Saturday afternoons. *Mailing address: P.O. Box 766, Mattituck, NY 11952

WLIM

WLIM, IN OPERATION since 1981, broadcasts at 10,000 watts. Visitors will have the opportunity to observe this radio station in full operation. Of special interest is the station's 9-foot (2.8-meter) satellite-receiving antenna. Network programs are transmitted via satellite by means of a digital system in which audio is converted into computer language and then reconverted to audio by WLIM's modern equipment.

Address/Telephone	*41 Pennsylvania Avenue Medford, NY 475-1580
When to Visit	Monday to Friday 10:00 a.m. to 4:00 p.m. By appointment

Charges/Fees	None
Suggested Grades	K–Adult
Guided Tour	Yes, by appointment
Maximum Group	12
Group Notice	2 to 3 weeks
Eating Facilities	None
Restroom Facilities	Yes
Handicapped Access	Yes
Additional Information	*Mailing address—Woodside Avenue, Patchogue, NY 11772

Schmitt Farm

VISITORS WILL OBSERVE the growing of garden vegetables and some farm animals. The tour includes a wagon ride, at the conclusion of which young visitors will go to the pumpkin field, where they may choose any pumpkin they wish. There is also a farm stand on the premises where farm-fresh vegetables may be purchased. Bring your camera. Photo comedy props available.

Address/Telephone	Exit 49 S (Walt Whitman Road) L.I. Expressway Melville, NY 11747 423-5693
When to Visit	October Monday to Friday 8:00 a.m. to 5:00 p.m. Weekends and Columbus Day—fields open to public
Charges/Fees	By arrangement
Suggested Grades	Pre-K–2
Guided Tour	None
Maximum Group	By arrangement
Group Notice	1 week
Eating Facilities	None
Restroom Facilities	Emergency only
Handicapped Access	No
Additional Information	Teachers should collect admission before visit.

WGSM

A T WGSM VISITORS will see newscasters and disc jockeys in action on the air. Also observed will be news programs in preparation as well as news service teletype facilities. Also on site are the facilities for WCTO, an FM station that is also included in the tour.

Address/Telephone	900 Walt Whitman Road
	Melville, NY 11747
	423-6740 Call: Mr. Woolf
When to Visit	By appointment
Charges/Fees	None
Suggested Grades	5–Adult
Guided Tour	Yes, 30 minutes
Maximum Group	15, with adequate supervision
Group Notice	3 weeks
Eating Facilities	None
Restroom Facilities	Yes
Handicapped Access	Yes

Miller Place Historical Museum
(Miller Place–Mount Sinai Historical Society)

T HE OLDEST SECTION of this colonial saltbox house dates back to 1720 and was originally built by William Miller. His descendants lived in it until the latter part of this century. Dr. Charles Millard, a Civil War surgeon, married into the Miller family and used this house for his medical practice. A display features Civil War medical instruments. Recently located on the property are the original Miller Place Post Office (c. 1820) and the Chereb barn (early 19th century), which is presently under reconstruction.

Address/Telephone	*North Country Road and Honey Lane
	Miller Place, NY 11764
	473-3449

When to Visit	By appointment
Charges/Fees	None
Suggested Grades	All ages
Guided Tour	Yes, by arrangement
Maximum Group	50 (in groups of 10)
Group Notice	2 weeks
Eating Facilities	None
Restroom Facilities	None
Handicapped Access	No
Additional Information	*Mailing address: Miller Place–Mount Sinai Historical Society, P.O. Box 651, Miller Place, NY 11764

Montauk Point Lighthouse Museum
(Montauk Historical Society)

THIS FAMOUS LIGHTHOUSE marks Long Island's easternmost tip. It stands on a high bluff and was constructed by order of George Washington. Actual construction of the lighthouse began on June 7, 1796 and it was put into operation in the spring of 1797. Originally maintained and operated by the U.S. Coast Guard, today only the light and foghorn are maintained and operated by the Montauk Historical Society.

Address/Telephone	*Montauk State Park Montauk, NY 11954 668-2544
When to Visit	Memorial Day to Labor Day: Sunday to Friday—10:30 a.m. to 6:00 p.m. May: Friday, Sunday and Monday—10:30 a.m. to 4:30 p.m. Saturday only—10:30 a.m. to 8:45 p.m. (until sunset in July and August) Call for off-season schedule
Charges/Fees	Adults—$2.50; children—$1.00

Montauk Point Lighthouse

Suggested Grades	4–Adult
Guided Tour	Yes, 30 minutes
Maximum Group	40
Group Notice	As much notice as possible
Eating Facilities	Picnic facilities and snack bar at State Park
Restroom Facilities	Yes, at State Park
Handicapped Access	Yes
Additional Information	Gift shop on premises Children must be at least 41″ tall to climb tower. *Mailing address: RFD #2, Box 112, Montauk, NY 11954

Pharaoh Site and Third House Museum

ARTIFACTS LEFT BEHIND by the native Montauks are on display in the museum along with a collection of aboriginal tools. Also displayed are a series of photographs of Teddy Roosevelt and the Roughriders, who trained in the area during the Spanish–American War. An educational display on archaeological techniques and dating methods is on display in the museum.

Address/Telephone	Montauk Highway
	Montauk, NY 11954
	852-7878 or 854-4949
When to Visit	Friday to Monday
	Memorial Day to Labor Day
	8:00 a.m. to 4:00 p.m.
	Schools and groups by special arrangement all year
Charges/Fees	None
Suggested Grades	3–Adult
Guided Tour	Yes, 30 minutes
Maximum Group	20
Group Notice	2 weeks
Eating Facilities	Picnic grounds
Restroom Facilities	Yes
Handicapped Access	No

Viking Ferry Line

WHETHER TRAVELING OVERSEA on the *Viking Starship* or *Viking Starliner*, visits can be made to New London or Block Island. These U.S. Coast Guard-inspected and licensed vessels are modern, up-to-date passenger ships with both indoor and outdoor seating. Whale-watching trips are available, July–September.

Address/Telephone	*West Lake Drive Montauk, NY 11954 668-5700
When to Visit	Call for schedule
Charges/Fees	Call for information
Suggested Grades	K–Adult, with adequate supervision
Guided Tour	None
Maximum Group	By arrangement
Group Notice	1 month
Eating Facilities	Restaurant on boat
Restroom Facilities	Yes
Handicapped Access	No
Additional Information	Bicycles transported for a fee *Mailing address: R.D. #1, Box 259, Montauk, NY 11954

Whale Watch and Natural History Tours
(Okeanos Ocean Research Foundation)

THE OKEANOS OCEAN Research Foundation offers several programs including environmental weekends with a Whale Watch Cruise aboard the roomy, 90-foot *Finback II,* which is licensed to carry 150 passengers. There are also slide/lecture presentations and field trips on the various aspects of marine and shoreline life. The Foundation represents New York State in the Mid-Atlantic Stranding Network and has been instrumental in rehabilitating and studying stranded marine mammals and sea turtles.

Address/Telephone	*Finback II, Viking Dock West Lake Drive Montauk, NY 11954 728-4522
When to Visit	Call or write for schedule and educational program brochure

Charges/Fees Call for information

Suggested Grades Varies with program—call

Guided Tour Call for arrangements

Maximum Group 150

Group Notice Groups: 6 weeks; Public: 2 weeks

Eating Facilities Full galley available

Restroom Facilities Yes

Handicapped Access No

Additional Information Dress appropriately according to weather. Warm, layered clothing advisable. Rubber-soled shoes are necessary. Motion-sickness medication advised.

*Mailing address: Box 776, Hampton Bays, NY 11946

Okeanos Ocean Research Foundation

Mount Sinai Marine Sanctuary Nature Center

THE CENTER OFFERS a number of fresh and saltwater displays highlighting Mount Sinai Harbor's ecosystems, and a large "touch" tank holding local marine life. Also on the grounds is Brookhaven's hard clam mariculture facility where clams are produced for release into town waters.

Address/Telephone	Harbor Beach Road
	Mount Sinai, NY 11766
	473-8346 or 654-7914
When to Visit	Daily
	June to September
	Call for current hours
	Groups: By special arrangement all year
Charges/Fees	None
Suggested Grades	K–Adult
Guided Tour	Yes, varies with program
Maximum Group	50
Group Notice	1 week
Eating Facilities	None
Restroom Facilities	Yes
Handicapped Access	Yes
Additional Information	Town *may* impose nonresident parking fee (Memorial Day to Labor Day).

Gemport Gallery

THIS GALLERY POSSESSES one of Long Island's largest collections of gems and minerals. On site, though not viewable by the public, jewelers work to incorporate these items into fine jewelry. These, as well as many gems and mineral specimens, are for sale to the public. New to the facility is a fluorescent mineral display which rivals that of most museums.

Address/Telephone	240 Route 25A Northport, NY 11768 261-8028
When to Visit	Daily: 10:00 a.m. to 6:00 p.m. Exceptions: Closes 9:00 p.m. Friday; opens noon Sunday Groups by appointment
Charges/Fees	None
Suggested Grades	5–Adult
Guided Tour	Yes
Maximum Group	15
Group Notice	2 weeks
Eating Facilities	None
Restroom Facilities	Emergency only
Handicapped Access	No

Northport Historical Museum

THIS MUSEUM FEATURES a permanent shipbuilding exhibit as well as displays of objects and memorabilia reflecting life in the Northport area through all periods of history. The education program offers classes for elementary school children. There is a gift shop on the premises that offers appropriate collectibles and publications.

Address/Telephone	215 Main Street Northport, NY 11768 757-9859
When to Visit	Tuesday to Sunday 1:00 p.m. to 4:30 p.m. Groups by appointment
Charges/Fees	Donation
Suggested Grades	5–Adult
Guided Tour	Summer walking tours of Main Street—Call for time and place—$1.50

Maximum Group	30
Group Notice	Call for arrangement
Eating Facilities	No
Restroom Facilities	Yes
Handicapped Access	No

BOCES Outdoor Environmental Education Program
(Connetquot River State Park Preserve)

THE 3,400 ACRES of Connetquot River State Park Preserve have been open to limited public access since August 1973. Prior to its acquisition by the State of New York, the property served as the site of the Southside Sportsman's Club for nearly a century. The club, described by a member as "an assembly of good-fellows," maintained the lands and waters for the protection and propagation of game birds, fish and wildlife. The Outdoor Learning Laboratory, presently located in the former main clubhouse, serves approximately 13,000 children each year.

Address/Telephone	*Connetquot River State Park Oakdale, NY 11769 581-6016
When to Visit	Monday to Friday 8:30 a.m. to 5:00 p.m. Summer and weekend programs by special arrangement. Environmental World Summer Program—parents call or write.
Charges/Fees	BOCES shared services aid available
Suggested Grades	Pre-K–Adult
Guided Tour	By request
Maximum Group	30

Group Notice	By April of previous school year
Eating Facilities	Indoor/outdoor—picnic or "brown bag"
Restroom Facilities	Yes
Handicapped Access	Yes
Additional Information	Write for literature
	*Mailing address: P.O. Box 254, Oakdale, NY 11769

Suffolk County Water Authority

VISITORS WILL BE given a tour of the SCWA's laboratory, the largest state-approved laboratory for the testing of drinking water in New York State. A member of the staff will describe the kinds of testing and equipment required to test water today and answer any questions the students may have. A visit can also be arranged to visit a pump station (well site) either in conjunction with a visit to the laboratory or as a separate field trip to a pump station in the vicinity of the school the students attend.

Address/Telephone	Sunrise Highway and Pond Road
	Oakdale, NY 11769
	589-5200, ext. 263
When to Visit	By appointment
Charges/Fees	None
Suggested Grades	3–12
Guided Tour	Tour of Laboratory—1 hour
	Tour of Laboratory and Pump Station—1½ to 2 hours
	Tour of Pump Station—1 hour
Maximum Group	15, with 2 adults
Group Notice	2 to 3 weeks
Eating Facilities	None
Restroom Facilities	Yes
Handicapped Access	No
Additional Information	Transportation to and from main office and to all nearby pump stations must be provided.

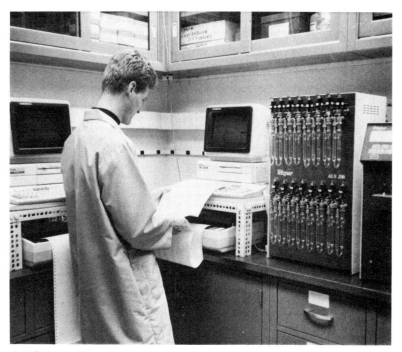

Suffolk County Water Authority

Flax Pond Marine Laboratory

THE LABORATORY IS a research and instructional facility operated by the Marine Science Research Center of SUNY at Stony Brook. Research is conducted on the biology and ecology of fish, crustaceans, mollusks and algae. The lab is located on Flax Pond, a 150-acre tidal wetlands preserve. There is a marked nature trail through the marsh with explanatory material available at the laboratory.

Address/Telephone *Crane Neck Road
Old Field, NY
632-8709

When to Visit	Lab: Monday to Friday—8:00 a.m. to 5:00 p.m.
	Marsh: Daily—Dawn to dusk
Charges/Fees	Lab—Call for information
	Marsh—Free
Suggested Grades	Lab—3–Adult
	Marsh—All ages
Guided Tour	Lab Tour—By arrangement
	Marsh Tour—Self-guided or guided by appointment
Maximum Group	Lab—30
	Marsh—Unlimited
Group Notice	Lab—2 weeks
	Marsh—None for self-guided tour
Eating Facilities	None
Restroom Facilities	Yes
Handicapped Access	No
Additional Information	Parking permit required: call 632-8709
	*Or write: Flax Pond Manager, Marine Science Research Center, SUNY, Stony Brook, NY 11794-5000

Museums of the Oysterponds Historical Society

THIS MUSEUM COMPLEX exhibits seven buildings. The Village House, a former inn, contains a Victorian parlor, local Indian artifacts, toys, period attire and local memorabilia. There are two one-room schoolhouses, one containing the Society's Genealogical and Archive library, and the other the Beach Plumb Museum shop. There is also a cookhouse, dormitory and The Red Barn, which houses horse-drawn vehicles, ice-harvesting equipment and a penny-candy store.

Address/Telephone	Village Lane
	Orient, NY 11957
	323-2480

When to Visit	Wednesday, Thursday, Saturday and Sunday—July and August Saturday and Sunday—September to June 2:00 p.m. to 5:00 p.m.
Charges/Fees	Adults—$3:00; children—$.50; children under 6—free
Suggested Grades	2–Adult
Guided Tour	Yes, for groups by arrangement
Maximum Group	30, with 2 adults
Group Notice	2 weeks
Eating Facilities	None
Restroom Facilities	Yes
Handicapped Access	No
Additional Information	Call only during visiting hours. Mail goes to Box 844 at the above address.

Lenz Winery

THE LENZ WINERY presents the visitor with 30 acres of grapes planted in the European tradition and a complex of award-winning buildings. One can see the small French oak barrels in which most of the wines are aged after fermenting in temperature-controlled stainless-steel tanks. Last season, six varieties of grapes were harvested to produce several varieties of wines, including Chardonnay, Merlot, Champagne, a red Bordeaux-style and a Gewürztraminer.

Address/Telephone	Main Road Peconic, NY 11958 734-6010
When to Visit	Daily 11:00 a.m. to 5:00 p.m.
Charges/Fees	None

Lenz Winery

GAYLE GLEASON

Suggested Grades	Not recommended for children
Guided Tour	Yes, 30 minutes
Maximum Group	30
Group Notice	2 weeks
Eating Facilities	None
Restroom Facilities	Yes
Handicapped Access	No

Pindar Vineyards

A COMPLETE VINEYARD and winery experience is offered at Pindar Vineyards. This interesting and educational tour will take the visitor from the first plantings of vines through the winery operation, showing every aspect of wine creation.

Address/Telephone	Main Road Peconic, NY 11958 734-6200
When to Visit	Daily except holidays 11:00 a.m. to 6:00 p.m.
Charges/Fees	None
Suggested Grades	4–Adult
Guided Tour	Yes, by arrangement
Maximum Group	100
Group Notice	1 month
Eating Facilities	None
Restroom Facilities	Yes
Handicapped Access	No

Mather House Museum
(Port Jefferson Historical Society)

THIS MUSEUM IS located in the homestead of the Mathers, a prominent shipbuilding family. The museum features a number of permanent exhibits, one of which highlights the harbor's early shipbuilding industry with displays of shipbuilding tools, models and photographs of early harbor activities. The museum complex includes a marine barn, toolshed, craft house, replicas of a country store, barber shop and butcher, and herb and perennial gardens.

Address/Telephone	*115 Prospect Street Port Jefferson, NY 11777 473-2665 or 928-6287 (Curator)

When to Visit	1:00 p.m. to 4:00 p.m.
	Saturday and Sunday—May 23 to June, and September 1 to Labor Day
	Tuesday, Wednesday, Saturday and Sunday—July and August
Charges/Fees	$1.00
Suggested Grades	K–Adult
Guided Tour	Yes—45 minutes
Maximum Group	35
Group Notice	2 weeks
Eating Facilities	None
Restroom Facilities	Yes
Handicapped Access	No
Additional Information	*Mailing address: Box 586, Port Jefferson, NY 11777

Theater Three

THEATER THREE IS Suffolk's only year-round professional theater. Theater Three presents eight Main Stage and four Second Stage productions each year, as well as seven fully staged, in-house children's musicals and five topical touring shows. It also offers an artist-in-residence program and drama classes for young people and adults.

Address/Telephone	*412 Main Street
	Port Jefferson, NY 11777
	Public: 928-9100 Group Sales: 928-9202
When to Visit	Call for schedule
Charges/Fees	Call for information
Suggested Grades	Pre-K–Adult, depending on production
Guided Tour	None
Maximum Group	425
Group Notice	1 month
Eating Facilities	None

Restroom Facilities	Yes
Handicapped Access	Limited handicapped facilities—call for further information.
Additional Information	Call for further information on touring theater programs.
	*Mailing address: P.O. Box 512, Port Jefferson, NY 11777

Old School House Museum

THIS SCHOOLHOUSE WAS built in 1822, cost $350 to build and was said at the time to be "the largest and best in Suffolk County." Its original location was at the edge of Quogue Street, somewhat west of its present site. The building was used as a schoolhouse and community meeting-place from 1822 until 1893. A collection of relics of Quogue's early history, farm and household implements, old letters, maps, collections of photographs and old toys are displayed.

Address/Telephone	*Quogue Street East Quogue, NY 11959 653-4224
When to Visit	July 1 to Labor Day Monday, Wednesday and Friday—2:00 p.m. to 5:00 p.m. Saturday—10:00 a.m. to noon
Charges/Fees	None
Suggested Grades	5–Adult
Guided Tour	None
Maximum Group	15
Group Notice	2 weeks
Eating Facilities	None
Restroom Facilities	At library for emergencies
Handicapped Access	No
Additional Information	*Mailing address: P.O. Box 1207, Quogue, NY 11959

Quogue Wildlife Refuge

THIS REFUGE CONTAINS 200 acres of varied natural and managed habitats encompassing the headwaters of Quantuck Creek in Quogue. Nature trails (which are wheelchair-accessible) reveal a wide cross section of ecological habitats, including ponds, swamp, freshwater bog, estuary and pine barrens. Located at the entrance to the refuge is a Distressed Wildlife Complex housing incapacitated birds and animals. These animals are cared for until they can be released into the wild.

Address/Telephone	Old Main Road and Old Country Road Quogue, NY 11959 653-4771
When to Visit	Daily 9:00 a.m. to 5:00 p.m.
Charges/Fees	None for individuals and families—only for groups wanting a guide, then by appointment
Suggested Grades	K–Adult
Guided Tour	For groups only; self-guiding trail for individuals and families
Maximum Group	45
Group Notice	1 week if possible
Eating Facilities	None
Restroom Facilities	Yes
Handicapped Access	Entire refuge is wheelchair-accessible
Additional Information	Nature Center with nature library and natural history exhibits open Tuesday, Thursday, Saturday and Sunday, 1:00 p.m. to 4:00 p.m. Ice Harvesting Museum with historical display of ice-cutting tools and methods.

Peconic Paddler

Canoe the Peconic River
(Peconic Paddler)

A CANOE TRIP along the Peconic River begins where the river is a very narrow stream at Connecticut Avenue in Calverton. When you approach the final destination near the traffic circle in the Village of Riverhead, you will have traveled through cranberry bogs and marshland and down waterfalls, and portaged three times. This river, which eventually empties into Flanders Bay, is primarily fed through the underground aquifer.

Address/Telephone   89 Peconic Avenue
Riverhead, NY 11901
727-9895

When to Visit   Monday to Friday—8:00 a.m., 10:00 a.m. and noon
Saturday and Sunday—(every half-hour) 8:00 a.m.
to 1:00 p.m.
Reservations recommended

Charges/Fees	$32.00—1 canoe
Suggested Grades	K–Adult—adequate supervision mandatory
Guided Tour	Map and instructions provided
Maximum Group	240
Group Notice	2 weeks
Eating Facilities	Picnic at appropriate sites along river. Restaurants at portage and Riverhead.
Restroom Facilities	Yes, at portage and Riverhead
Handicapped Access	No
Additional Information	Life jackets and paddles provided

Hallockville Museum Farm

L OCATED ON EASTERN Long Island's scenic North Fork, the Hallockville Museum Farm is a two-and-one-half acre complex of original 18th- and 19th-century farm buildings, including the c. 1765 Hallock Homestead, a large barn, a shoemaker's shop, workshop, smokehouse and outhouse. Occupied for nearly 200 years by five generations of the Hallock family, the site is one of the oldest intact farms on Long Island and is listed on the National Register of Historic Places. Open year-round, we offer tours, permanent and temporary exhibits, craft demonstrations, festivals, school programs, workshops, lectures and much more!

Address/Telephone	163 Sound Avenue Riverhead, NY 11901 298-5292
When to Visit	Wednesday to Sunday 10:00 a.m. to 4:00 p.m.
Charges/Fees	Adults—$2.50; children—$1.50
Suggested Grades	K–Adult
Guided Tour	Orientation—followed by self-guided tour
Maximum Group	40
Group Notice	3 weeks
Eating Facilities	Yes, picnic facilities
Restroom Facilities	Yes, handicapped-accessible
Handicapped Access	No

Long Island Horticultural Research Laboratory
(Cornell University)

THE LONG ISLAND Horticultural Research Laboratory is a site where applied agricultural research is conducted on vegetables, grapes, nursery and greenhouse plants and turfgrass. Plant problems such as diseases, weeds, and insects are investigated as part of the overall program.

Address/Telephone	39 Sound Avenue Riverhead, NY 11901 727-3595
When to Visit	Tours on a scheduled basis only. Groups wishing to visit should write or phone Coordinator's Office.
Charges/Fees	None
Suggested Grades	8–Adult
Guided Tour	Yes, 1 hour in length, including an informal talk regarding experiments in progress at the time
Maximum Group	30
Group Notice	2 weeks
Eating Facilities	None
Restroom Facilities	Emergency only
Handicapped Access	No

Splish Splash
(Long Island's Water Activity Park)

THE FIRST OF its kind on Long Island, this 100-percent-water activity park opened in 1991. This 40-acre facility features a variety of water activities such as slides and waterways for tube rides. For mom and dad, or the less daring, there is a 1,300-foot long "Lazy River" to cruise on with a tube. For the leisure set, there is a sunbathing area.

Address/Telephone	2549 Middle Country Road Riverhead, NY 11901 727-3600
When to Visit	Weekends and holidays—mid-May to mid-June Daily—mid-June to first week in September
Charges/Fees	Call for information
Suggested Grades	All ages
Guided Tour	Yes
Maximum Group	None
Group Notice	Yes, at least 24 hours in advance
Eating Facilities	Restaurant featuring hot dogs, deli sandwiches and pizza
Restroom Facilities	Yes
Handicapped Access	No

Suffolk County Courts

THIS TRIP OFFERS young people a special lecture on the criminal justice system and court systems of New York State and Suffolk County. A visit to an operating courtroom is part of the tour. Depending on the calendar of courtroom activities for the day, students may witness courtroom procedures such as jury selection and jury trials.

Address/Telephone	Griffing Avenue Riverhead, NY 11901 852-2365 Call: Mr. Markowitz, Public Information Officer
When to Visit	Monday to Friday 9:30 a.m. to 12:45 p.m. By special appointment only
Charges/Fees	None
Suggested Grades	11–Adult
Guided Tour	Yes, 3 hours—arrive 9:30 a.m., leave 12:30 p.m.
Maximum Group	25

Group Notice	As much as possible. Schedule fills up months in advance.
Eating Facilities	None
Restroom Facilities	Yes
Handicapped Access	Yes
Additional Information	Call above and also Suffolk County Bar Association (864-1800) for guest speakers to schools. Pamphlet supplied to all students during visit. It is suggested that lower-grade levels utilize the District Courts for visitations and programs.

Suffolk County Historical Society

THE SUFFOLK COUNTY Historical Society's collections, exhibitions and programs concentrate on the history of Suffolk County and its people. The combined resources of the museum, research library and archives and education programs uniquely enable the Society to bring Suffolk County history to life for visitors of all ages. The Society offers a variety of programs for visiting school groups along with programs for adults and children throughout the year.

Address/Telephone	300 West Main Street (Route 25) Riverhead, NY 11901 727-2881
When to Visit	Tuesday to Saturday 12:30 p.m. to 4:30 p.m. Groups and morning visits by appointment
Charges/Fees	None
Suggested Grades	K–Adult
Guided Tour	Yes, 1 hour
Maximum Group	30
Group Notice	2 weeks
Eating Facilities	None
Restroom Facilities	Yes
Handicapped Access	No

Suffolk County Legislature

VISITORS WILL HAVE the opportunity to observe the 18-member Suffolk County Legislature debate, formulate and pass or defeat proposed laws and spending bills. The Legislature also holds many legal and public hearings as well as public presentations. Depending on the business of the day, opportunities may present themselves to visit and discuss governmental problems with local representatives and other County officials.

Address/Telephone	Riverhead County Center Riverhead, NY 11901 853-5000
	William H. Rogers Legislature Building Hauppauge County Center Veterans' Memorial Highway Hauppauge, NY 11788
When to Visit	Meetings alternate between Hauppauge and Riverhead. Call for further information.
Charges/Fees	None
Suggested Grades	7–Adult
Guided Tour	Yes, tour of County facilities by arrangement
Maximum Group	30
Group Notice	1 week
Eating Facilities	Yes
Restroom Facilities	Yes
Handicapped Access	Yes
Additional Information	Call to arrange for seminars and special programs. Also call for scheduled "mock legislature" sessions that students take part in (duration—40 minutes).

Suffolk County Maximum Security Facility

VISITS TO THE Suffolk County Maximum Security Facility are offered under the Y.E.S. (Youth Enlightenment Seminar) Program. The program is designed to serve as a learning experience for Criminal Justice classes from Suffolk County. The program utilizes the negative realities of incarceration to serve as a deterrent for adolescents who might be prone to criminal behavior in the future.

Address/Telephone	100 Center Drive Riverhead, NY 11901 852-8038
When to Visit	By appointment
Charges/Fees	None
Suggested Grades	8–Adult
Guided Tour	Yes, 2½ hours
Maximum Group	By arrangement
Group Notice	Make reservations well in advance
Eating Facilities	None
Restroom Facilities	Yes
Handicapped Access	Yes
Additional Information	In order to participate in this program, contact Community Relations. The Sheriff's office also provides presentations suitable for classrooms and school assemblies for grades K–12.

Custom House

IN 1789, SAG HARBOR became a United States Port of Entry. This building was the first Custom House in New York State and the first post office on Long Island. The furnishings illustrate the sophisticated Eastern lifestyle of the period, including many Dering and other Sag Harbor family pieces and pictures.

Custom House

Address/Telephone	Garden Street Sag Harbor, NY 11963 941-9444 Call: Society for the Preservation of Long Island Antiquities
When to Visit	Tuesday to Sunday June to September 10:00 a.m. to 5:00 p.m. Groups by appointment
Charges/Fees	Adults—$2.00; children—$1.00; children under 6—free Call for group rates
Suggested Grades	2–Adult
Guided Tour	Yes, 40 minutes
Maximum Group	By arrangement
Group Notice	2 weeks
Eating Facilities	None
Restroom Facilities	Yes
Handicapped Access	No
Additional Information	Do not touch antiques.

Elizabeth Morton Wildlife Refuge

T HIS 187-ACRE REFUGE is one of over 470 refuges throughout the United States that provide wintering, resting and nesting areas for waterfowl and protect endangered and other wildlife. It is a nesting stop for piping plover (which are listed on the Federal Endangered Species list). Sandy, gravelly and rocky beaches fringe the peninsula and the wooded bluffs of the neck overlook Peconic and Noyac Bays. The remainder is woodland, brush and open fields.

Address/Telephone	*Noyac Road Sag Harbor, NY 11963 286-0485, 725-2270 (summer only)
When to Visit	Daily ½ hour before sunrise to ½ hour after sunset
Charges/Fees	None
Suggested Grades	K–Adult
Guided Tour	No. However, 10-minute orientations are available. Arrangements in advance are required.
Maximum Group	30
Group Notice	Call ahead
Eating Facilities	None
Restroom Facilities	Yes
Handicapped Access	No
Additional Information	Location: Three miles west of Sag Harbor on north shore of southern fork on Noyac Road. *Mailing address: P.O. Box 21, Shirley, NY 11967

Sag Harbor Whaling and Historical Museum

A S YOU ENTER this museum you will pass through the bones of a right whale. These genuine jawbones were brought home by a Sag Harbor whaler and have been on display for over 100 years. The museum covers the history of whaling on Long Island over the last century. It displays logs recording the voyages of ships, whaling equipment, scrimshaw, period furniture and ship models.

Address/Telephone	*Main Street Sag Harbor, NY 11963 725-0770 or 725-1094
When to Visit	May to October 1 Monday to Saturday—10:00 a.m. to 5:00 p.m. Sunday—1:00 p.m. to 5:00 p.m.
Charges/Fees	Adults—$2.00; children—$.75; seniors—$1.50
Suggested Grades	3–Adult—call for group rates
Guided Tour	By appointment
Maximum Group	50
Group Notice	3 weeks
Eating Facilities	Picnic facilities
Restroom Facilities	Yes
Handicapped Access	Handicap ramp available
Additional Information	Historian available at museum. *Mailing address: Box 1327, Sag Harbor, NY 11963

Islip Grange
(Town of Islip)

THE ISLIP GRANGE is a 12-acre mini-restoration village dedicated to preserving Long Island-based structures that were threatened with demolition. The restoration includes original houses and cottages, a water-pumping windmill, a barn and outbuildings. The grounds are often used for arts and crafts fairs.

Address/Telephone	10 Broadway Avenue Sayville, NY 11782 472-7016
When to Visit	Monday to Thursday 9:00 a.m. to 5:00 p.m. Other dates available to groups by appointment

Charges/Fees	None
Suggested Grades	3–Adult
Guided Tour	Self-guided tour
Maximum Group	30
Group Notice	1 week
Eating Facilities	None, "brown bag"
Restroom Facilities	Yes
Handicapped Access	No
Additional Information	Call or write for schedule of arts and crafts fairs

The Thompson House
(Society for the Preservation of Long Island Antiquities)

B UILT IN 1700, the Thompson House offers a vivid portrait of 18th-century family life and customs on Long Island. Unusually large with superb early architectural details, it houses one of the finest collections of early Long Island furniture. The North Suffolk Garden Club maintains a Colonial herb garden.

Address/Telephone	93 North Country Road Setauket, NY 11733 941-9444 Call: Society for the Preservation of Long Island Antiquities
When to Visit	Saturday and Sunday May to October 1:00 p.m. to 5:00 p.m.
Charges/Fees	Adults—$1.50; children and seniors—$1.00 Call for school discovery brochure and fees
Suggested Grades	2–Adult
Guided Tour	Yes, 45 minutes
Maximum Group	By arrangement

Group Notice	2 weeks
Eating Facilities	None
Restroom Facilities	None
Handicapped Access	No
Additional Information	Annual Herb Festival held on grounds in June. Brochure available.

The Mashomack Preserve
(The Nature Conservancy)

THE MASHOMACK PRESERVE consists of 2,000 acres of oak woodlands, marshes, freshwater ponds and interlacing tidal creeks, edged in white by 10 miles of coastline. This green peninsula still hosts ibis and hummingbirds, muskrats and foxes, harbor seals and terrapins. Together with nearby Gardiners Island, the Mashomack area supports one of the East Coast's largest concentrations of nesting osprey. Its woods and wetland harbor rare plants, native orchids, lichens and a variety of ferns and clubmosses. There is a gift shop that also houses small displays.

Address/Telephone	*79 South Ferry Road Shelter Island, NY 11964 748-1001
When to Visit	Wednesday to Monday 9:00 a.m. to 5:00 p.m.
Charges/Fees	Adults—$1.50; children—$1.00
Suggested Grades	K–Adult
Guided Tour	Yes, by arrangement. 1 to 2½ hours for groups of 10 or more
Maximum Group	30
Group Notice	2 weeks
Eating Facilities	None
Restroom Facilities	Yes
Handicapped Access	Yes
Additional Information	*Mailing address: P.O. Box 850, Shelter Island, NY 11964

Old Havens House
(Shelter Island Historical Society)

BUILT C. 1743 with a mid-19th-century addition, the Old Havens House served as a residence, post office and general store. Four of the rooms have been decorated with early 19th-century furnishings by the D.A.R. Many parts of the original construction have been left exposed for inspection. There is also a children's museum room featuring toys, dolls and youth furniture.

Address/Telephone	16 South Ferry Road (Route 114) Shelter Island, NY 11964 749-0025
When to Visit	Thursday mornings Saturday and Sunday—Noon to 4:00 p.m. (summer months) Other hours by appointment
Charges/Fees	$1.50
Suggested Grades	4–Adult
Guided Tour	Yes, 30 minutes to 1 hour
Maximum Group	30
Group Notice	1 week
Eating Facilities	None
Restroom Facilities	Yes (not for groups)
Handicapped Access	No
Additional Information	It is advisable to call ahead before visiting

BOCES Outdoor Environmental Education Program
(Caleb Smith State Park Preserve)

THE 543-ACRE CALEB Smith State Park Preserve is one of the last tracts of undeveloped land on Long Island and is a refuge for organisms displaced by the rapid and extensive growth of suburbia. Botanically, the park maintains a high diversity of over 200 plant species composing several plant communities. The Program is held in a reconstructed 120-year-old barn and stable with a prefabricated unit added to the main structure.

Address/Telephone	BOCES Outdoor Environmental Education Program Caleb Smith State Park 810 Meadow Road Smithtown, NY 11787 360-3652 or 360-3671
When to Visit	Monday to Friday 8:30 a.m. to 5:00 p.m. Summer and weekend programs by special arrangement
Charges/Fees	BOCES shared service aid available
Suggested Grades	Pre-K–Adult
Guided Tour	By request
Maximum Group	1 learning unit (30 students)
Group Notice	By April of previous school year
Eating Facilities	Indoor-outdoor—picnic or "brown bag"
Restroom Facilities	Yes
Handicapped Access	Yes
Additional Information	Write for literature

Caleb Smith House
(Smithtown Historical Society)

THE CALEB SMITH House, presently located on Smithtown's Village Green, was originally built in 1819 and located on Jericho Turnpike in Commack. The House now serves as a headquarters for the Smithtown Historical Society and a repository for documents and books relating to the history of Smithtown. Artifacts of local interest, including pieces of furniture once owned by the Smith and Blydenburgh families, are on display.

Caleb Smith House

Address/Telephone	North Country and Middle Country Roads Smithtown, NY 11787 265-6768
When to Visit	Monday to Friday (all year)—9:00 a.m. to 4:00 p.m. Saturday—Noon to 4:00 p.m. Groups by appointment only
Charges/Fees	Adults—$1.00; children—$.25
Suggested Grades	2–Adult
Guided Tour	Yes, 30 minutes
Maximum Group	30, with adequate supervision
Group Notice	2 weeks
Eating Facilities	None
Restroom Facilities	Yes
Handicapped Access	No
Additional Information	Consignment shop with linens, antiques, collectibles, china and crystal

Epnetus Smith Tavern
(Smithtown Historical Society)

THE WEST WING of this building dates back to 1690. The Inn was added c. 1750. Moved three times from its original site, the building accommodated British troops during the Revolution and, in more recent times, the Smithtown Library.

Address/Telephone	211 E. Middle Country Road Smithtown, NY 11787 265-6768
When to Visit	Schools and groups only, by appointment
Charges/Fees	$3.00
Suggested Grades	2–Adult
Guided Tour	Program only
Maximum Group	30
Group Notice	1 week
Eating Facilities	"Brown bag"
Restroom Facilities	Yes
Handicapped Access	Yes
Additional Information	Special school program on the role of the tavern in life in early America, by arrangement

Franklin O. Arthur Farm
(Smithtown Historical Society)

PRESENTLY MANAGED BY the Smithtown Historical Society, the Franklin O. Arthur House was built sometime between 1730 and 1750. With hopes of opening the facility as a farm museum in the not too distant future, the Society at present uses the house as a learning center for schools and youth groups. The barn has in storage an interesting collection of old-time sleighs and buggies.

Address/Telephone	245 E. Middle Country Road Smithtown, NY 11787 265-6768
When to Visit	By appointment
Charges/Fees	School program—$3.00 per child
Suggested Grades	4–Adult
Guided Tour	Program only
Maximum Group	30
Group Notice	Book early in September
Eating Facilities	"Brown bag"
Restroom Facilities	Yes
Handicapped Access	Yes
Additional Information	Hands-on Colonial craft program, emphasizing fiber preparation, dyeing, spinning and weaving

Judge J. Lawrence Smith Homestead
(Smithtown Historical Society)

BUILT C. 1835 and currently under restoration, the Homestead was the residence and law office of Judge Lawrence Smith. The law office and library are being restored with Judge Smith's personal properties on display. Restoration is ongoing.

Address/Telephone	205 E. Middle Country Road Smithtown, NY 11787 265-6768
When to Visit	Contact Smithtown Historical Society
Charges/Fees	Donation
Suggested Grades	4–Adult
Guided Tour	By arrangement
Maximum Group	30
Group Notice	2 weeks
Eating Facilities	None
Restroom Facilities	Yes
Handicapped Access	No

Richard H. Handley Long Island History Room
(Smithtown Library)

THE HANDLEY LONG ISLAND History Room is the repository for an important collection of books, pamphlets, newspapers, photographs, manuscripts and maps relating to Long Island and the Town of Smithtown. Included are genealogies of many Long Island families.

Address/Telephone	One North Country Road Smithtown, NY 11787 265-2072
When to Visit	Tuesday—10:00 a.m. to 1:00 p.m. and 2:00 p.m. to 6:00 p.m. Wednesday—1:00 p.m. to 5:00 p.m. and 6:00 p.m. to 9:00 p.m. Thursday and Friday—10:00 a.m. to 1:00 p.m. and 2:00 p.m. to 6:00 p.m. Saturday—10:00 a.m. to 1:00 p.m. and 2:00 p.m. to 5:00 p.m. School groups by appointment
Charges/Fees	None
Suggested Grades	4–Adult (children under grade 9 should be supervised by adults)
Guided Tour	Workshops by arrangement
Maximum Group	12
Group Notice	1 week
Eating Facilities	None
Restroom Facilities	Yes
Handicapped Access	Yes
Additional Information	Materials are for use in the library only.

Parrish Art Museum

Parrish Art Museum

ESTABLISHED IN 1898, this museum provides numerous cultural pro-grams for eastern Suffolk communities. Included are lectures, adult and children's workshops, jazz concerts, classical music concerts and children's theater. The permanent collection includes 19th-century etchings and American art, with extensive holdings of works by William Merritt Chase and Fairfield Porter.

Address/Telephone	25 Job's Lane Southampton, NY 11968 283-2118
When to Visit	Wednesday to Monday—Spring, Summer and Fall Thursday to Monday—Winter 10:00 a.m. to 5:00 p.m. Exception: Sunday—1:00 p.m. to 5:00 p.m.

Charges/Fees	$2.00
Suggested Grades	Varies with program, call in advance
Guided Tour	Yes
Maximum Group	35
Group Notice	1 week
Eating Facilities	None
Restroom Facilities	Yes
Handicapped Access	Wheelchair access available
Additional Information	Museum shop

Southampton Historical Museum
(Southampton Colonial Society)

ERECTED ON THE site of original farmland granted to William Rogers in 1645, this museum exhibits sea captains' memorabilia, Shinnecock and Montauk Indian artifacts, a country store, post office, schoolhouse, a barn and a working blacksmith's shop.

Address/Telephone	17 Meeting House Lane
	Southampton, NY 11968
	283-0605 Call: Mrs. Hansen
	283-1612 Call: Mr. Keene
When to Visit	Tuesday to Sunday
	mid-June to mid-September
	11:00 a.m. to 5:00 p.m.
Charges/Fees	Adults—$2.00; children—$.50
Suggested Grades	K–Adult
Guided Tour	None
Maximum Group	50, with 1 adult per group of 8
Group Notice	2 weeks
Eating Facilities	None
Restroom Facilities	Yes
Handicapped Access	Yes

Southampton Hospital

THIS 194-BED NONPROFIT acute-care medical center occupies a 10-acre tract one quarter-mile from the ocean in this rural resort community. Its modern equipment includes magnetic resonance imaging (MRI), a computerized axial tomography (CAT) scanner, nuclear medicine, echocardiography, ultra sonography, intensive and cardiac care units, complete with patient monitoring systems, six fully equipped operating rooms, a birthing room and coverage by a medical staff of over 100 physicians, including every major medical specialty.

Address/Telephone	240 Meeting House Lane Southampton, NY 11968 283-4404 Call: Community Relations
When to Visit	Monday to Friday By appointment
Charges/Fees	None
Suggested Grades	7–Adult
Guided Tour	Yes, 1 hour
Maximum Group	12
Group Notice	2 weeks
Eating Facilities	Coffee shop
Restroom Facilities	Yes
Handicapped Access	Yes

Thomas Halsey Homestead
(Southampton Colonial Society)

THE HALSEY HOMESTEAD is considered to be the oldest English frame house in New York State. Built in 1648 by Thomas Halsey, one of the original settlers of Southampton, it contains furnishings of the 17th and 18th centuries. An herb garden is located on the property.

Address/Telephone	South Main Street Southampton, NY 11968 283-0605 Call: Mrs. Hansen
When to Visit	Tuesday to Sunday Mid-June to mid-September 11:00 a.m. to 4:30 p.m.
Charges/Fees	Adults—$2.00; children 6 to 12—$.50; children under 6—free
Suggested Grades	9–Adult
Guided Tour	None. Considerable information provided by hostess
Maximum Group	10
Group Notice	2 weeks
Eating Facilities	None
Restroom Facilities	Emergency only
Handicapped Access	No

Custer Institute

THE INSTITUTE HAS an astronomical observatory containing a 6″ Eichner refractor, a 5″ Alvan Clark refractor, a 3-meter radio telescope, an auditorium, library, small museum, lens-grinding workshop and exhibits. In addition to astronomy, programs include such topics as economics, philosophy, ecology, music and the arts. Some meetings are open to members only, but frequently the public is invited to an evening of stargazing or a program of classic films, concerts, art exhibits, etc. The observatory is open to the public most Saturday nights, weather permitting.

Address/Telephone	P.O. Box 1204 Main Bay View Road Southold, NY 11971 765-2626
When to Visit	Call 722-3850 or 744-4318 for appointment

Charges/Fees	Donation
Suggested Grades	7–Adult
Guided Tour	Yes, up to 2 hours, by appointment
Maximum Group	30
Group Notice	2 weeks
Eating Facilities	Picnic facilities
Restroom Facilities	Yes
Handicapped Access	No
Additional Information	Write for most recent schedule of programs and activities: Barbara Lebkuecher, Treas., Herricks Lane, Box 645, Jamesport, NY 11947

Horton Point Lighthouse
Marine Museum
(Southold Historical Society)

BUILT 1856, FIRST lit 1857. Its third-order light, moved to a skeletal structure in 1933, was returned to its tower and recommissioned by the U.S. Coast Guard in 1990. Overlooking Long Island Sound, the building and property, owned by Southold Park District, have been cooperatively restored with the Southold Historical Society, which operates the Marine Museum. Horton Point Lighthouse is the most accessible of the six lighthouses in the Town of Southold.

Address/Telephone	Southold Historical Society Lighthouse Road Southold, NY 11971 765-5500 (weekdays, 10:00 a.m. to 2:00 p.m.)
	Lighthouse 765-2101 (weekend hours) 765-3262 (special requests)

Horton Point Lighthouse   VALENTINE RUCH

When to Visit	Saturday and Sunday May 30 to October 12 11:30 a.m. to 4:00 p.m.
Charges/Fees	Museum: Adults—$1.00; children—free Tower: Adults—$.50; children—free
Suggested Grades	3–Adult
Guided Tour	Yes, 30 minutes
Maximum Group	40, with adequate supervision
Group Notice	2 weeks
Eating Facilities	Picnic facilities
Restroom Facilities	Yes
Handicapped Access	No
Additional Information	Film-viewing room, outdoor concerts, etc. Please call for information.

Southold Historical Museum
(Southold Historical Society)

SOUTHOLD, FOUNDED IN 1640, was the first English-speaking settle-
ment on Long Island. The Southold Historical Society operates a
museum in which the main Victorian house contains an art gallery, a
millinery room and a collection of dolls, toys and period furniture. Also on
site are the Thomas Moore pre-Revolutionary house, the Pine Neck Barn,
a carriage house, blacksmith shop, The Buttery, complete with utensils,
and the Old Bayview Schoolhouse.

Address/Telephone	Main Road
	Southold, NY 11971
	765-5500
When to Visit	Saturday and Sunday
	July and August
	1:00 p.m. to 4:00 p.m.
Charges/Fees	Donation
Suggested Grades	K–Adult
Guided Tour	Yes, 1 hour
Maximum Group	30, with adequate supervision
Group Notice	2 weeks
Eating Facilities	Picnic facilities nearby
Restroom Facilities	Yes
Handicapped Access	No
Additional Information	Museum shop next block

Southold Indian Museum
(The Incorporated Long Island Chapter, New York State Archaeological Association)

THIS ARCHAEOLOGICAL MUSEUM houses one of the most complete
collections of Algonquin artifacts to be found on Long Island. One
exhibit displays the numerous varieties of corn grown by local Indians,
another displays collections of spears and arrowheads. There is also the

largest collection of restored Algonquin ceramic pottery. The museum collection contains over 300,000 artifacts (not all on display at one time).

Address/Telephone	P.O. Box 268
	Main Bay View Road
	Southold, NY 11971
	765-5577
When to Visit	Sunday
	1:30 p.m. to 4:30 p.m.
	Groups by arrangement
Charges/Fees	$1.00
Suggested Grades	Pre-K–Adult (special craft program for grades 4–6 in August)
Guided Tour	Yes, 1 hour
Maximum Group	40 (By special arrangement, larger groups can be accommodated)
Group Notice	4 weeks
Eating Facilities	None
Restroom Facilities	Yes
Handicapped Access	No

Merrill Lake Sanctuary
(The Nature Conservancy)

THE SANCTUARY HOSTS an exemplary accessible salt-marsh community, with both low and high marsh zones. Largely covered with plant life, at high tide the marsh is sometimes flooded with salt water. It also serves as a nursery for fish and wildlife. There is a self-guided trail with an explanatory booklet illustrating plants and wildlife found at the salt marsh. There are several nesting osprey at the Sanctuary.

Address/Telephone	*Fire Place Road and Hog Creek Road
	Springs (East Hampton), NY 11937
	725-2936
When to Visit	Daily
	Sunrise to sunset

Charges/Fees	None
Suggested Grades	K–Adult
Guided Tour	Yes, 60 to 90 minutes—2 weeks notice needed
Maximum Group	20
Group Notice	4 weeks
Eating Facilities	None
Restroom Facilities	None
Handicapped Access	No
Additional Information	Talk may be arranged at main office, call 725-2936. *Mailing address: P.O. Box 2694, Sag Harbor, NY 11963

Wicks Farm and Garden

GROUPS ARE FREE to tour greenhouses that grow Easter, Christmas and spring annuals. Festive seasons offer wide displays of goblins, witches, turkeys, Colonial and Christmas characters and other objects when appropriate. The most popular time for children at the Wicks Farm and Garden is during the Halloween pumpkin picking and witch and goblin time from mid-September through October 31st.

Address/Telephone	445 North Country Road (Route 25A) St. James, NY 11780 584-5727
When to Visit	Halloween Season—September 15 to October 31 Christmas Season—Thanksgiving to New Year's Day 10:00 a.m. to 5:00 p.m. Schools and groups: Call for appointment
Charges/Fees	Call for information
Suggested Grades	Pre-K–Adult
Guided Tour	Self-guided tour of greenhouses
Maximum Group	Unlimited

Group Notice	1 month
Eating Facilities	None
Restroom Facilities	None
Handicapped Access	Yes
Additional Information	Festive seasons and holidays offer special displays. Mini-displays offered during lesser holidays.

Museum of Long Island Natural Sciences

"MAN AND NATURE on Long Island" is the theme of this museum and the thrust of its educational programs. Reflecting the exhibit and object strengths of the museum, programs emphasize shore processes and the relationship of organisms, including man, with the coast. All are examined in a temporal, historical and geographical context. There are special weekend classes and lectures for families and adults and after-school children's programs.

Address/Telephone	Earth and Space Science Building SUNY Stony Brook, NY 11794 632-8230
When to Visit	Monday to Friday 9:00 a.m. to 4:00 p.m.
Charges/Fees	Public—free; groups—by arrangement
Suggested Grades	K–Adult
Guided Tour	None
Maximum Group	60
Group Notice	2 weeks
Eating Facilities	None
Restroom Facilities	Yes
Handicapped Access	Yes
Additional Information	Special course offerings for educators

Museums at Stony Brook

Museums at Stony Brook

THIS NINE-ACRE SITE is devoted to American art, history and horse-drawn transportation. Three exhibit buildings display the work of William Sidney Mount (1807–1868) and other American artists, over 90 horse-drawn carriages, miniature rooms, antique decoys and changing exhibitions on a variety of historical themes. Also on hand: blacksmith shop, one-room schoolhouse, carriage shed, 1794 barn and Museum Store.

Address/Telephone   1208 North Country Road (Route 25A)
Stony Brook, NY 11794
751-0066

When to Visit	Wednesday to Saturday and most Monday holidays—10:00 a.m. to 5:00 p.m. Sunday—Noon to 5:00 p.m. Open daily July and August
Charges/Fees	Adults—$6.00; students and seniors—$4.00; children 6–12—$3.00; children under 6 and museum members—free
Suggested Grades	K–Adult
Guided Tour	Yes, call for special appointment
Maximum Group	35
Group Notice	2 weeks
Eating Facilities	Picnic facilities
Restroom Facilities	Yes
Handicapped Access	Yes
Additional Information	Special education programs available

Staller Center for the Arts
(The University at Stony Brook)

WITH ITS FIVE theaters and 4,700-square-foot art gallery, the Staller Center is the only comprehensive center for the arts of Long Island. The Center is open year-round and offers world-class attractions in music, film, ballet, theater, the visual arts and lectures. In the summer it is the venue for the International Theater Festival and the Bach Aria Festival and Institute.

Address/Telephone	Stony Brook, NY 11794 632-7235 (tours) 632-7230 (ticket/performance information)
When to Visit	Call or write for schedule
Charges/Fees	Varies with program
Suggested Grades	All ages depending on program
Guided Tour	By special arrangement only
Maximum Group	Varies with program

Group Notice	2 weeks
Eating Facilities	Yes
Restroom Facilities	Yes
Handicapped Access	Yes
Additional Information	Many performances free or voluntary donation

University Art Gallery at Stony Brook
(The University at Stony Brook)

THE UNIVERSITY ART Gallery, located in the Staller Center for the Arts at the State University of New York at Stony Brook, is a double-storied, 4,700-square-foot facility with 200 running feet of wall space. The gallery presents six exhibitions of 20th-century art each year.

Address/Telephone	Stony Brook, NY 11794 632-7240
When to Visit	Tuesday to Saturday Noon to 4:00 p.m. Also open to the public prior to some evening performances at the Staller Center for the Arts.
Charges/Fees	None
Suggested Grades	K–Adult
Guided Tour	By arrangement
Maximum Group	40
Group Notice	2 weeks
Eating Facilities	None
Restroom Facilities	Yes
Handicapped Access	Yes

Brookhaven National Laboratory
(Exhibit Center/Science Museum)

EXPLORE THE MARVELS of science and learn about Brookhaven National Laboratory; participatory exhibits, audio-visual presentations, historic collections in a three-story decommissioned nuclear reactor; shake hands with a skeleton, whisper around a corner, and see yourself in the mirror hall.

Address/Telephone	Upton, NY 11973
	282-2345
When to Visit	Sunday—July and August, except holidays
	10:00 a.m. to 3:00 p.m.
	Schools and groups: programs by appointment
Charges/Fees	None
Suggested Grades	K–Adult
Guided Tour	Yes, length depends on program
Maximum Group	By arrangement
Group Notice	3 weeks
Eating Facilities	Cafeteria open by special arrangement for school groups
Restroom Facilities	Yes
Handicapped Access	Handicapped access to first floor only

Le Reve

EXPERIENCE AWARD-WINNING wines in an extraordinary French Normandy château. The winery is situated on 40 acres of vineyards and features tours and tastings daily. Learn about the centuries-old process of winemaking with state-of-the-art equipment.

Address/Telephone	162 Montauk Highway
	Water Mill, NY 11976
	726-7555

When to Visit	Daily
	Memorial Day through October
	Noon to 5:00 p.m. (on the hour) for tours and wine tasting
Charges/Fees	None
Suggested Grades	K–Adult
Guided Tour	Yes, 30 minutes
Maximum Group	250
Group Notice	1 week
Eating Facilities	Picnic facilities available
Restroom Facilities	Yes
Handicapped Access	Yes
Additional Information	Call for special events and program calendar

Old Water Mill Museum

THIS GRISTMILL IS the oldest operating water mill on Long Island. Water-driven, it houses tools of a miller, cooper, carpenter, blacksmith, wheelwright, weaver and spinner. The exhibits encourage viewer participation—you may try the mortar and pestle, turn wooden gears and use a fanning mill. Corn meal ground at the mill is available. Art exhibits.

Address/Telephone	Old Mill Road (off Route 27)
	Water Mill, NY 11976
	726-4625
When to Visit	Memorial Day to Labor Day
	Thursday to Saturday, and Monday—11:00 a.m. to 5:00 p.m.
	Sunday—1:00 p.m. to 5:00 p.m.
	Groups by appointment
Charges/Fees	Donation
Suggested Grades	K–Adult
Guided Tour	Yes, 40 minutes
Maximum Group	40

Group Notice	1 week
Eating Facilities	None
Restroom Facilities	Yes
Handicapped Access	No
Additional Information	Call in advance

Babylon Resource Recovery Facility

THE BABYLON RESOURCE Recovery Facility is a high tech, state-of-the-art facility designed to incinerate solid waste for the purpose of producing steam and electricity. Unprocessed municipal waste is delivered to this facility, where it undergoes a mass-burn process. There is little or no sorting of the waste prior to incineration. In simpler terms, this process uses garbage as a fuel and burns it to recover energy through thermal recycling.

Address/Telephone	125 Gleam Street West Babylon, NY 11704 491-1776
When to Visit	Monday to Friday 10:00 a.m. to 4:00 p.m. Also, by special appointment
Charges/Fees	None
Suggested Grades	4–Adult
Guided Tour	Yes, 2 hours
Maximum Group	30
Group Notice	2 weeks
Eating Facilities	None
Restroom Facilities	Yes
Handicapped Access	Yes
Additional Information	Do not wear high heels when visiting this facility.

Southwest Sewer District at Bergen Point

VISITORS WILL OBSERVE the largest water-treatment plant utilizing primary and secondary treatment of liquid sewage wastes in Suffolk County. It is designed to treat over 30 million gallons of waste water per day, producing a clear effluent free of harmful or objectionable materials and meeting all federal requirements. Other trips to facilities utilizing different processes at the University at Stony Brook and the County Centers at Hauppauge and Yaphank can also be arranged through Bergen Point.

Address/Telephone	600 Bergen Avenue West Babylon, NY 11704 854-4150
When to Visit	Tuesday, Wednesday and Thursday March to November By appointment only
Charges/Fees	None
Suggested Grades	9–Adult
Guided Tour	Yes, 1 hour
Maximum Group	20, with 1 adult per group of 10
Group Notice	2 weeks
Eating Facilities	None
Restroom Facilities	Yes
Handicapped Access	No
Additional Information	By calling the telephone number above, visits to additional facilities (SUNY/Stony Brook, Yaphank, Hauppauge) with different processes can be arranged.

Sagtikos Manor

LOUIS DORMAND

Sagtikos Manor

A T THE HOUSE, the original part of which was constructed in 1692, visitors will observe many items of historical significance. Furnishings and a style of living for the well-to-do during the Revolutionary period are available for study. The house was occupied by British General Sir Henry Clinton during the American Revolution and was included in the tour of Long Island by President Washington.

Address/Telephone   *Montauk Highway
West Bay Shore, NY 11706
661-8348

When to Visit   Wednesday, Thursday and Sunday—July and
      August
Groups by appointment—June to September
1:00 p.m. to 4:00 p.m.

Charges/Fees	Adults—$3.00; children—$1.00
	School groups: students—free; adults—$3.00
Suggested Grades	3–Adult
Guided Tour	Yes, 45 minutes
Maximum Group	60, with 1 adult per group of 8
Group Notice	2 weeks
Eating Facilities	Yes, picnic on porch and backyard
Restroom Facilities	Yes
Handicapped Access	No
Additional Information	*Mailing address: Sagtikos Manor, P.O. Box P-344, Bay Shore, NY 11706

Community Museum at West Islip

THIS MUSEUM HOUSES a collection of photographs of some of the area's oldest homes, antique agricultural equipment, Colonial flags, oil lamps, an antique hand-crocheted spread depicting U.S. presidents through Grant and early West Islip newspapers. A display of prize ribbons won by poultry and livestock raised on the Arnold Estate brings back memories of the time of West Islip's gentlemen farmers. Indian artifacts, including arrowheads and stone axes, highlight our Indian heritage (the Secatogues). Glass fishing floats recall our fishing and maritime past.

Address	90 Higbie Lane
	West Islip, NY 11795
When to Visit	Wednesdays and Sundays
	1:00 p.m. to 3:00 p.m.
Charges/Fees	Donation
Suggested Grades	All ages
Guided Tour	By appointment
Maximum Group	10
Group Notice	By arrangement
Eating Facilities	None
Restroom Facilities	Yes
Handicapped Access	No

Suffolk Marine Museum

S TEP BACK IN time and appreciate the maritime activities of Long Island while enjoying a panoramic view of Great South Bay. This museum contains permanent maritime exhibits, a library for serious maritime-history students, a multi-image/sound show about oysters and two Long Island-built oystering vessels docked next to the historic oyster house. It also includes Long Island's largest small-craft collection.

Address/Telephone	*Montauk Highway West Sayville, NY 11796 854-4974
When to Visit	Wednesday to Saturday—10:00 a.m. to 3:00 p.m. Sunday—Noon to 4:00 p.m.
Charges/Fees	Donation
Suggested Grades	4–Adult
Guided Tour	Yes
Maximum Group	50, with 2 adults
Group Notice	2 weeks, make reservations
Eating Facilities	Picnic facilities
Restroom Facilities	Yes
Handicapped Access	Yes
Additional Information	*Mailing address: 86 West Avenue, P.O. Box 184, West Sayville, NY 11796

Suffolk County Emergency Management Office

A TRIP TO this facility will show the visitor an emergency shelter and a communications system that will serve as a central coordination center in the event of disasters and emergencies. The Suffolk County Emergency Management Office is the alternate seat of the County government in the event of an emergency.

Address/Telephone	*E.O.C. Building C0110 Yaphank Avenue Yaphank, NY 11980 852-4900
When to Visit	By appointment
Charges/Fees	None
Suggested Grades	1–Adult
Guided Tour	Yes, ½ hour to 2 hours including film and talk
Maximum Group	40
Group Notice	1 week
Eating Facilities	None
Restroom Facilities	Yes
Handicapped Access	Yes
Additional Information	*Mailing address: P.O. Box 127, Yaphank Avenue, E.O.C. Building C0110, Yaphank, NY 11980-0127

Suffolk County Farm and Education Center

THE SUFFOLK COUNTY Farm and Education Center, managed by Cornell Cooperative Extension of Suffolk County, offers a unique opportunity for families and groups to see a real working farm with cattle, pigs, hens, turkeys and other domesticated animals, and a historic haybarn built in 1871. There are also daily hayrides in July and August, and on weekends in the spring and fall.

Address/Telephone	*Yaphank Avenue Yaphank, NY 11980 852-4611
When to Visit	Daily 9:00 a.m. to 3:00 p.m. Call for schedule
Charges/Fees	Public—free; groups—by arrangement
Suggested Grades	Pre-K–Adult
Guided Tour	Yes, by appointment
Maximum Group	By arrangement

Group Notice	1 month—general public needs no reservations
Eating Facilities	Picnic facilities available on request
Restroom Facilities	Yes
Handicapped Access	Yes
Additional Information	Call for information on workshops, classes, special-occasion programs and special events. Free brochure/calendar of events.

*Mailing address: P.O. Box 129, Yaphank, NY 11980-0129

ADDENDA

Cradle of Aviation Museum
[NASSAU COUNTY]

HOUSED IN TWO 1932 hangars at the former Mitchel Air Force Base, the Museum portrays the aerospace heritage of Long Island. Thus far, over forty aircraft and spacecraft, mostly built on Long Island, have been collected. In the near future, the Museum is to be renovated into a world-class air/space museum, including an advanced large-screen Omnimax theatre.

Address/Telephone	Mitchel Field Garden City, NY 11530 222-1191
When to visit	Seasonal, call for schedule
Charges/Fees	Varies with program
Suggested Grades	K–Adult
Guided Tour	Yes, 1 hour, groups only by arrangement
Maximum Group	100
Group Notice	2 weeks
Eating Facilities	None
Restroom Facilities	Yes
Handicapped Access	Yes
Additional Information	Call for schedule, events and to observe progress of renovation.

Long Beach
[NASSAU COUNTY]

A SOUTH SHORE WATERFRONT resort and residential community with a wide sandy beach and boardwalk open to the public. The City of Long Beach is known for its wide variety of ethnic restaurants.

Address/Telephone	Long Beach Chamber of Commerce 350 National Boulevard Long Beach, NY 11561 432-6000
When to Visit	Daily Lifeguards on duty 8:30 a.m. to 6:00 p.m. Beach officially opens June 28
Charges/Fees	Adults—$5.00; children under 13—free Free parking (though not plentiful)
Guided Tour	None
Maximum Group	Unlimited
Group Notice	None
Eating Facilities	Boardwalk with concession stands
Restrooms	Yes
Handicapped Access	Yes
Additional Information	Directions to Long Beach (barrier island): Follow Meadowbrook Causeway, Atlantic Beach Bridge or Long Beach Bridge to Pacific Boulevard to Ohio Avenue.

Jones Beach State Park
[NASSAU COUNTY]

WHAT MAY BE Long Island's most celebrated beach complex is located on the South Shore near Wantagh, approximately 35 miles from New York City. Swimming in eight Atlantic Ocean bathing areas and Zachs Bay. East and West Bathhouses feature Olympic-size pools, diving areas and wading pools. In addition, each bathhouse includes lockers and showers for the convenience of pool and ocean bathers.

Fishermen delight in the many types of fishing available. A bait station and fishing piers can be used for bay fishing at Field 10, while beach areas at West End 2 and Field 6 are designated for surf casting (by permit). The West End Boat Basin (east of Jones Inlet) offers daytime berths, pump-out station, mooring area, comfort stations and refreshment stand.

Surfboarding is permitted at the West End 2 area from the Monday after Thanksgiving through Labor Day. There is a 1½-mile-long boardwalk with deck games, softball fields, roller skating, fitness course, dancing nightly at bandshell, concerts, special events, miniature golf and basketball.

Address/Telephone	Jones Beach State Park Wantagh, NY 11793 785-1600
When to Visit	Daily Sunrise to sunset Swimming from Memorial Day to Labor Day
Charges/Fees	$4.00 per car—Memorial Day to Labor Day
Guided Tour	None
Maximum Group	Write (see below) or call for information
Group Notice	Write (see below) or call for information
Eating Facilities	Picnic areas, boardwalk with concession stands, Jones Beach Restaurant
Restroom Facilities	Yes
Handicapped Access	Yes
Additional Information	Applications for group outing permits for all Long Island State Park facilities may be obtained by sending a stamped, self-addressed envelope to: Group Outings, P.O. Box 247, Babylon, NY 11702. Allow 10 days from date of postmark for processing of permit.

CATEGORY INDEX

ALPHABETICAL INDEX

This is a strict alphabetization by exact full title of facility
(only opening "The"'s are omitted).

A CATALOG OF SELECTED
DOVER BOOKS
IN ALL FIELDS OF INTEREST

A CATALOG OF SELECTED DOVER
BOOKS IN ALL FIELDS OF INTEREST

CONCERNING THE SPIRITUAL IN ART, Wassily Kandinsky. Pioneering work by father of abstract art. Thoughts on color theory, nature of art. Analysis of earlier masters. 12 illustrations. 80pp. of text. 5⅜ × 8½. 23411-8 Pa. $3.95

ANIMALS: 1,419 Copyright-Free Illustrations of Mammals, Birds, Fish, Insects, etc., Jim Harter (ed.). Clear wood engravings present, in extremely lifelike poses, over 1,000 species of animals. One of the most extensive pictorial sourcebooks of its kind. Captions. Index. 284pp. 9 × 12. 23766-4 Pa. $11.95

CELTIC ART: The Methods of Construction, George Bain. Simple geometric techniques for making Celtic interlacements, spirals, Kells-type initials, animals, humans, etc. Over 500 illustrations. 160pp. 9 × 12. (USO) 22923-8 Pa. $8.95

AN ATLAS OF ANATOMY FOR ARTISTS, Fritz Schider. Most thorough reference work on art anatomy in the world. Hundreds of illustrations, including selections from works by Vesalius, Leonardo, Goya, Ingres, Michelangelo, others. 593 illustrations. 192pp. 7⅛ × 10¼. 20241-0 Pa. $8.95

CELTIC HAND STROKE-BY-STROKE (Irish Half-Uncial from "The Book of Kells"): An Arthur Baker Calligraphy Manual, Arthur Baker. Complete guide to creating each letter of the alphabet in distinctive Celtic manner. Covers hand position, strokes, pens, inks, paper, more. Illustrated. 48pp. 8¼ × 11. 24336-2 Pa. $3.95

EASY ORIGAMI, John Montroll. Charming collection of 32 projects (hat, cup, pelican, piano, swan, many more) specially designed for the novice origami hobbyist. Clearly illustrated easy-to-follow instructions insure that even beginning papercrafters will achieve successful results. 48pp. 8¼ × 11. 27298-2 Pa. $2.95

THE COMPLETE BOOK OF BIRDHOUSE CONSTRUCTION FOR WOOD-WORKERS, Scott D. Campbell. Detailed instructions, illustrations, tables. Also data on bird habitat and instinct patterns. Bibliography. 3 tables. 63 illustrations in 15 figures. 48pp. 5¼ × 8½. 24407-5 Pa. $1.95

BLOOMINGDALE'S ILLUSTRATED 1886 CATALOG: Fashions, Dry Goods and Housewares, Bloomingdale Brothers. Famed merchants' extremely rare catalog depicting about 1,700 products: clothing, housewares, firearms, dry goods, jewelry, more. Invaluable for dating, identifying vintage items. Also, copyright-free graphics for artists, designers. Co-published with Henry Ford Museum & Greenfield Village. 160pp. 8¼ × 11. 25780-0 Pa. $9.95

HISTORIC COSTUME IN PICTURES, Braun & Schneider. Over 1,450 costumed figures in clearly detailed engravings—from dawn of civilization to end of 19th century. Captions. Many folk costumes. 256pp. 8⅜ × 11¾. 23150-X Pa. $10.95

STICKLEY CRAFTSMAN FURNITURE CATALOGS, Gustav Stickley and L. & J. G. Stickley. Beautiful, functional furniture in two authentic catalogs from 1910. 594 illustrations, including 277 photos, show settles, rockers, armchairs, reclining chairs, bookcases, desks, tables. 183pp. 6½ × 9¼.   23838-5 Pa. $8.95

AMERICAN LOCOMOTIVES IN HISTORIC PHOTOGRAPHS: 1858 to 1949, Ron Ziel (ed.). A rare collection of 126 meticulously detailed official photographs, called "builder portraits," of American locomotives that majestically chronicle the rise of steam locomotive power in America. Introduction. Detailed captions. xi + 129pp. 9 × 12.   27393-8 Pa. $12.95

AMERICA'S LIGHTHOUSES: An Illustrated History, Francis Ross Holland, Jr. Delightfully written, profusely illustrated fact-filled survey of over 200 American lighthouses since 1716. History, anecdotes, technological advances, more. 240pp. 8 × 10¾.   25576-X Pa. $11.95

TOWARDS A NEW ARCHITECTURE, Le Corbusier. Pioneering manifesto by founder of "International School." Technical and aesthetic theories, views of industry, economics, relation of form to function, "mass-production split" and much more. Profusely illustrated. 320pp. 6⅛ × 9¼. (USO)   25023-7 Pa. $8.95

HOW THE OTHER HALF LIVES, Jacob Riis. Famous journalistic record, exposing poverty and degradation of New York slums around 1900, by major social reformer. 100 striking and influential photographs. 233pp. 10 × 7⅞.
22012-5 Pa $10.95

FRUIT KEY AND TWIG KEY TO TREES AND SHRUBS, William M. Harlow. One of the handiest and most widely used identification aids. Fruit key covers 120 deciduous and evergreen species; twig key 160 deciduous species. Easily used. Over 300 photographs. 126pp. 5⅜ × 8½.   20511-8 Pa. $3.95

COMMON BIRD SONGS, Dr. Donald J. Borror. Songs of 60 most common U.S. birds: robins, sparrows, cardinals, bluejays, finches, more—arranged in order of increasing complexity. Up to 9 variations of songs of each species.
Cassette and manual 99911-4 $8.95

ORCHIDS AS HOUSE PLANTS, Rebecca Tyson Northen. Grow cattleyas and many other kinds of orchids—in a window, in a case, or under artificial light. 63 illustrations. 148pp. 5⅜ × 8½.   23261-1 Pa. $3.95

MONSTER MAZES, Dave Phillips. Masterful mazes at four levels of difficulty. Avoid deadly perils and evil creatures to find magical treasures. Solutions for all 32 exciting illustrated puzzles. 48pp. 8¼ × 11.   26005-4 Pa. $2.95

MOZART'S DON GIOVANNI (DOVER OPERA LIBRETTO SERIES), Wolfgang Amadeus Mozart. Introduced and translated by Ellen H. Bleiler. Standard Italian libretto, with complete English translation. Convenient and thoroughly portable—an ideal companion for reading along with a recording or the performance itself. Introduction. List of characters. Plot summary. 121pp. 5¼ × 8½.
24944-1 Pa. $2.95

TECHNICAL MANUAL AND DICTIONARY OF CLASSICAL BALLET, Gail Grant. Defines, explains, comments on steps, movements, poses and concepts. 15-page pictorial section. Basic book for student, viewer. 127pp. 5⅜ × 8½.
21843-0 Pa. $3.95

BRASS INSTRUMENTS: Their History and Development, Anthony Baines. Authoritative, updated survey of the evolution of trumpets, trombones, bugles, cornets, French horns, tubas and other brass wind instruments. Over 140 illustrations and 48 music examples. Corrected and updated by author. New preface. Bibliography. 320pp. 5⅜ × 8½. 27574-4 Pa. $9.95

HOLLYWOOD GLAMOR PORTRAITS, John Kobal (ed.). 145 photos from 1926–49. Harlow, Gable, Bogart, Bacall; 94 stars in all. Full background on photographers, technical aspects. 160pp. 8⅜ × 11¼. 23352-9 Pa. $9.95

MAX AND MORITZ, Wilhelm Busch. Great humor classic in both German and English. Also 10 other works: "Cat and Mouse," "Plisch and Plumm," etc. 216pp. 5⅜ × 8½. 20181-3 Pa. $5.95

THE RAVEN AND OTHER FAVORITE POEMS, Edgar Allan Poe. Over 40 of the author's most memorable poems: "The Bells," "Ulalume," "Israfel," "To Helen," "The Conqueror Worm," "Eldorado," "Annabel Lee," many more. Alphabetic lists of titles and first lines. 64pp. 5$\frac{3}{16}$ × 8¼. 26685-0 Pa. $1.00

SEVEN SCIENCE FICTION NOVELS, H. G. Wells. The standard collection of the great novels. Complete, unabridged. First Men in the Moon, Island of Dr. Moreau, War of the Worlds, Food of the Gods, Invisible Man, Time Machine, In the Days of the Comet. Total of 1,015pp. 5⅜ × 8½. (USO) 20264-X Clothbd. $29.95

AMULETS AND SUPERSTITIONS, E. A. Wallis Budge. Comprehensive discourse on origin, powers of amulets in many ancient cultures: Arab, Persian, Babylonian, Assyrian, Egyptian, Gnostic, Hebrew, Phoenician, Syriac, etc. Covers cross, swastika, crucifix, seals, rings, stones, etc. 584pp. 5⅜ × 8½. 23573-4 Pa. $12.95

RUSSIAN STORIES/PYCCKNE PACCKA3bl: A Dual-Language Book, edited by Gleb Struve. Twelve tales by such masters as Chekhov, Tolstoy, Dostoevsky, Pushkin, others. Excellent word-for-word English translations on facing pages, plus teaching and study aids, Russian/English vocabulary, biographical/critical introductions, more. 416pp. 5⅜ × 8½. 26244-8 Pa. $8.95

PHILADELPHIA THEN AND NOW: 60 Sites Photographed in the Past and Present, Kenneth Finkel and Susan Oyama. Rare photographs of City Hall, Logan Square, Independence Hall, Betsy Ross House, other landmarks juxtaposed with contemporary views. Captures changing face of historic city. Introduction. Captions. 128pp. 8¼ × 11. 25790-8 Pa. $9.95

AIA ARCHITECTURAL GUIDE TO NASSAU AND SUFFOLK COUNTIES, LONG ISLAND, The American Institute of Architects, Long Island Chapter, and the Society for the Preservation of Long Island Antiquities. Comprehensive, well-researched and generously illustrated volume brings to life over three centuries of Long Island's great architectural heritage. More than 240 photographs with authoritative, extensively detailed captions. 176pp. 8¼ × 11. 26946-9 Pa. $14.95

NORTH AMERICAN INDIAN LIFE: Customs and Traditions of 23 Tribes, Elsie Clews Parsons (ed.). 27 fictionalized essays by noted anthropologists examine religion, customs, government, additional facets of life among the Winnebago, Crow, Zuni, Eskimo, other tribes. 480pp. 6⅛ × 9¼. 27377-6 Pa. $10.95

FRANK LLOYD WRIGHT'S HOLLYHOCK HOUSE, Donald Hoffmann. Lavishly illustrated, carefully documented study of one of Wright's most controversial residential designs. Over 120 photographs, floor plans, elevations, etc. Detailed perceptive text by noted Wright scholar. Index. 128pp. 9¼ × 10¾.
27133-1 Pa. $11.95

THE MALE AND FEMALE FIGURE IN MOTION: 60 Classic Photographic Sequences, Eadweard Muybridge. 60 true-action photographs of men and women walking, running, climbing, bending, turning, etc., reproduced from rare 19th-century masterpiece. vi + 121pp. 9 × 12. 24745-7 Pa. $10.95

1001 QUESTIONS ANSWERED ABOUT THE SEASHORE, N. J. Berrill and Jacquelyn Berrill. Queries answered about dolphins, sea snails, sponges, starfish, fishes, shore birds, many others. Covers appearance, breeding, growth, feeding, much more. 305pp. 5¼ × 8¼. 23366-9 Pa. $7.95

GUIDE TO OWL WATCHING IN NORTH AMERICA, Donald S. Heintzelman. Superb guide offers complete data and descriptions of 19 species: barn owl, screech owl, snowy owl, many more. Expert coverage of owl-watching equipment, conservation, migrations and invasions, etc. Guide to observing sites. 84 illustrations. xiii + 193pp. 5⅜ × 8½. 27344-X Pa. $7.95

MEDICINAL AND OTHER USES OF NORTH AMERICAN PLANTS: A Historical Survey with Special Reference to the Eastern Indian Tribes, Charlotte Erichsen-Brown. Chronological historical citations document 500 years of usage of plants, trees, shrubs native to eastern Canada, northeastern U.S. Also complete identifying information. 343 illustrations. 544pp. 6½ × 9¼. 25951-X Pa. $12.95

STORYBOOK MAZES, Dave Phillips. 23 stories and mazes on two-page spreads: Wizard of Oz, Treasure Island, Robin Hood, etc. Solutions. 64pp. 8¼ × 11.
23628-5 Pa. $2.95

NEGRO FOLK MUSIC, U.S.A., Harold Courlander. Noted folklorist's scholarly yet readable analysis of rich and varied musical tradition. Includes authentic versions of over 40 folk songs. Valuable bibliography and discography. xi + 324pp. 5⅜ × 8½. 27350-4 Pa. $7.95

MOVIE-STAR PORTRAITS OF THE FORTIES, John Kobal (ed.). 163 glamor, studio photos of 106 stars of the 1940s: Rita Hayworth, Ava Gardner, Marlon Brando, Clark Gable, many more. 176pp. 8⅜ × 11¼. 23546-7 Pa. $10.95

BENCHLEY LOST AND FOUND, Robert Benchley. Finest humor from early 30s, about pet peeves, child psychologists, post office and others. Mostly unavailable elsewhere. 73 illustrations by Peter Arno and others. 183pp. 5⅜ × 8½.
22410-4 Pa. $5.95

YEKL and THE IMPORTED BRIDEGROOM AND OTHER STORIES OF YIDDISH NEW YORK, Abraham Cahan. Film Hester Street based on Yekl (1896). Novel, other stories among first about Jewish immigrants on N.Y.'s East Side. 240pp. 5⅜ × 8½. 22427-9 Pa. $5.95

SELECTED POEMS, Walt Whitman. Generous sampling from *Leaves of Grass.* Twenty-four poems include "I Hear America Singing," "Song of the Open Road," "I Sing the Body Electric," "When Lilacs Last in the Dooryard Bloom'd," "O Captain! My Captain!"—all reprinted from an authoritative edition. Lists of titles and first lines. 128pp. 5³/₁₆ × 8¼. 26878-0 Pa. $1.00

THE BEST TALES OF HOFFMANN, E. T. A. Hoffmann. 10 of Hoffmann's most important stories: "Nutcracker and the King of Mice," "The Golden Flowerpot," etc. 458pp. 5⅜ × 8½. 21793-0 Pa. $8.95

FROM FETISH TO GOD IN ANCIENT EGYPT, E. A. Wallis Budge. Rich detailed survey of Egyptian conception of "God" and gods, magic, cult of animals, Osiris, more. Also, superb English translations of hymns and legends. 240 illustrations. 545pp. 5⅜ × 8½. 25803-3 Pa. $11.95

FRENCH STORIES/CONTES FRANÇAIS: A Dual-Language Book, Wallace Fowlie. Ten stories by French masters, Voltaire to Camus: "Micromegas" by Voltaire; "The Atheist's Mass" by Balzac; "Minuet" by de Maupassant; "The Guest" by Camus, six more. Excellent English translations on facing pages. Also French-English vocabulary list, exercises, more. 352pp. 5⅜ × 8½. 26443-2 Pa. $8.95

CHICAGO AT THE TURN OF THE CENTURY IN PHOTOGRAPHS: 122 Historic Views from the Collections of the Chicago Historical Society, Larry A. Viskochil. Rare large-format prints offer detailed views of City Hall, State Street, the Loop, Hull House, Union Station, many other landmarks, circa 1904–1913. Introduction. Captions. Maps. 144pp. 9⅜ × 12¼. 24656-6 Pa. $12.95

OLD BROOKLYN IN EARLY PHOTOGRAPHS, 1865–1929, William Lee Younger. Luna Park, Gravesend race track, construction of Grand Army Plaza, moving of Hotel Brighton, etc. 157 previously unpublished photographs. 165pp. 8⅞ × 11¾. 23587-4 Pa. $12.95

THE MYTHS OF THE NORTH AMERICAN INDIANS, Lewis Spence. Rich anthology of the myths and legends of the Algonquins, Iroquois, Pawnees and Sioux, prefaced by an extensive historical and ethnological commentary. 36 illustrations. 480pp. 5⅜ × 8½. 25967-6 Pa. $8.95

AN ENCYCLOPEDIA OF BATTLES: Accounts of Over 1,560 Battles from 1479 B.C. to the Present, David Eggenberger. Essential details of every major battle in recorded history from the first battle of Megiddo in 1479 B.C. to Grenada in 1984. List of Battle Maps. New Appendix covering the years 1967–1984. Index. 99 illustrations. 544pp. 6½ × 9¼. 24913-1 Pa. $14.95

SAILING ALONE AROUND THE WORLD, Captain Joshua Slocum. First man to sail around the world, alone, in small boat. One of great feats of seamanship told in delightful manner. 67 illustrations. 294pp. 5⅜ × 8½. 20326-3 Pa. $5.95

ANARCHISM AND OTHER ESSAYS, Emma Goldman. Powerful, penetrating, prophetic essays on direct action, role of minorities, prison reform, puritan hypocrisy, violence, etc. 271pp. 5⅜ × 8½. 22484-8 Pa. $5.95

MYTHS OF THE HINDUS AND BUDDHISTS, Ananda K. Coomaraswamy and Sister Nivedita. Great stories of the epics; deeds of Krishna, Shiva, taken from puranas, Vedas, folk tales; etc. 32 illustrations. 400pp. 5⅜ × 8½. 21759-0 Pa. $9.95

BEYOND PSYCHOLOGY, Otto Rank. Fear of death, desire of immortality, nature of sexuality, social organization, creativity, according to Rankian system. 291pp. 5⅜ × 8½. 20485-5 Pa. $7.95

A THEOLOGICO-POLITICAL TREATISE, Benedict Spinoza. Also contains unfinished Political Treatise. Great classic on religious liberty, theory of government on common consent. R. Elwes translation. Total of 421pp. 5⅜ × 8½. 20249-6 Pa. $7.95

MY BONDAGE AND MY FREEDOM, Frederick Douglass. Born a slave, Douglass became outspoken force in antislavery movement. The best of Douglass' autobiographies. Graphic description of slave life. 464pp. 5⅜ × 8½.   22457-0 Pa. $8.95

FOLLOWING THE EQUATOR: A Journey Around the World, Mark Twain. Fascinating humorous account of 1897 voyage to Hawaii, Australia, India, New Zealand, etc. Ironic, bemused reports on peoples, customs, climate, flora and fauna, politics, much more. 197 illustrations. 720pp. 5⅜ × 8½.   26113-1 Pa. $15.95

THE PEOPLE CALLED SHAKERS, Edward D. Andrews. Definitive study of Shakers: origins, beliefs, practices, dances, social organization, furniture and crafts, etc. 33 illustrations. 351pp. 5⅜ × 8½.   21081-2 Pa. $7.95

THE MYTHS OF GREECE AND ROME, H. A. Guerber. A classic of mythology, generously illustrated, long prized for its simple, graphic, accurate retelling of the principal myths of Greece and Rome, and for its commentary on their origins and significance. With 64 illustrations by Michelangelo, Raphael, Titian, Rubens, Canova, Bernini and others. 480pp. 5⅜ × 8½.   27584-1 Pa. $9.95

PSYCHOLOGY OF MUSIC, Carl E. Seashore. Classic work discusses music as a medium from psychological viewpoint. Clear treatment of physical acoustics, auditory apparatus, sound perception, development of musical skills, nature of musical feeling, host of other topics. 88 figures. 408pp. 5⅜ × 8½. 21851-1 Pa. $9.95

THE PHILOSOPHY OF HISTORY, Georg W. Hegel. Great classic of Western thought develops concept that history is not chance but rational process, the evolution of freedom. 457pp. 5⅜ × 8½.   20112-0 Pa. $8.95

THE BOOK OF TEA, Kakuzo Okakura. Minor classic of the Orient: entertaining, charming explanation, interpretation of traditional Japanese culture in terms of tea ceremony. 94pp. 5⅜ × 8½.   20070-1 Pa. $2.95

LIFE IN ANCIENT EGYPT, Adolf Erman. Fullest, most thorough, detailed older account with much not in more recent books, domestic life, religion, magic, medicine, commerce, much more. Many illustrations reproduce tomb paintings, carvings, hieroglyphs, etc. 597pp. 5⅜ × 8½.   22632-8 Pa. $9.95

SUNDIALS, Their Theory and Construction, Albert Waugh. Far and away the best, most thorough coverage of ideas, mathematics concerned, types, construction, adjusting anywhere. Simple, nontechnical treatment allows even children to build several of these dials. Over 100 illustrations. 230pp. 5⅜ × 8½. 22947-5 Pa. $5.95

DYNAMICS OF FLUIDS IN POROUS MEDIA, Jacob Bear. For advanced students of ground water hydrology, soil mechanics and physics, drainage and irrigation engineering, and more. 335 illustrations. Exercises, with answers. 784pp. 6⅛ × 9¼.   65675-6 Pa. $19.95

SONGS OF EXPERIENCE: Facsimile Reproduction with 26 Plates in Full Color, William Blake. 26 full-color plates from a rare 1826 edition. Includes "The Tyger," "London," "Holy Thursday," and other poems. Printed text of poems. 48pp. 5¼ × 7.
24636-1 Pa. $3.95

OLD-TIME VIGNETTES IN FULL COLOR, Carol Belanger Grafton (ed.). Over 390 charming, often sentimental illustrations, selected from archives of Victorian graphics—pretty women posing, children playing, food, flowers, kittens and puppies, smiling cherubs, birds and butterflies, much more. All copyright-free. 48pp. 9¼ × 12¼.   27269-9 Pa. $5.95

PERSPECTIVE FOR ARTISTS, Rex Vicat Cole. Depth, perspective of sky and sea, shadows, much more, not usually covered. 391 diagrams, 81 reproductions of drawings and paintings. 279pp. 5⅜ × 8½. 22487-2 Pa. $6.95

DRAWING THE LIVING FIGURE, Joseph Sheppard. Innovative approach to artistic anatomy focuses on specifics of surface anatomy, rather than muscles and bones. Over 170 drawings of live models in front, back and side views, and in widely varying poses. Accompanying diagrams. 177 illustrations. Introduction. Index. 144pp. 8⅜ × 11¼. 26723-7 Pa. $7.95

GOTHIC AND OLD ENGLISH ALPHABETS: 100 Complete Fonts, Dan X. Solo. Add power, elegance to posters, signs, other graphics with 100 stunning copyright-free alphabets: Blackstone, Dolbey, Germania, 97 more—including many lower-case, numerals, punctuation marks. 104pp. 8⅛ × 11. 24695-7 Pa. $7.95

HOW TO DO BEADWORK, Mary White. Fundamental book on craft from simple projects to five-bead chains and woven works. 106 illustrations. 142pp. 5⅜ × 8. 20697-1 Pa. $4.95

THE BOOK OF WOOD CARVING, Charles Marshall Sayers. Finest book for beginners discusses fundamentals and offers 34 designs. "Absolutely first rate . . . well thought out and well executed."—E. J. Tangerman. 118pp. 7¾ × 10⅝. 23654-4 Pa. $5.95

ILLUSTRATED CATALOG OF CIVIL WAR MILITARY GOODS: Union Army Weapons, Insignia, Uniform Accessories, and Other Equipment, Schuyler, Hartley, and Graham. Rare, profusely illustrated 1846 catalog includes Union Army uniform and dress regulations, arms and ammunition, coats, insignia, flags, swords, rifles, etc. 226 illustrations. 160pp. 9 × 12. 24939-5 Pa. $10.95

WOMEN'S FASHIONS OF THE EARLY 1900s: An Unabridged Republication of "New York Fashions, 1909," National Cloak & Suit Co. Rare catalog of mail-order fashions documents women's and children's clothing styles shortly after the turn of the century. Captions offer full descriptions, prices. Invaluable resource for fashion, costume historians. Approximately 725 illustrations. 128pp. 8⅜ × 11¼. 27276-1 Pa. $10.95

THE 1912 AND 1915 GUSTAV STICKLEY FURNITURE CATALOGS, Gustav Stickley. With over 200 detailed illustrations and descriptions, these two catalogs are essential reading and reference materials and identification guides for Stickley furniture. Captions cite materials, dimensions and prices. 112pp. 6½ × 9¼. 26676-1 Pa. $9.95

EARLY AMERICAN LOCOMOTIVES, John H. White, Jr. Finest locomotive engravings from early 19th century: historical (1804–74), main-line (after 1870), special, foreign, etc. 147 plates. 142pp. 11⅜ × 8¼. 22772-3 Pa. $8.95

THE TALL SHIPS OF TODAY IN PHOTOGRAPHS, Frank O. Braynard. Lavishly illustrated tribute to nearly 100 majestic contemporary sailing vessels: Amerigo Vespucci, Clearwater, Constitution, Eagle, Mayflower, Sea Cloud, Victory, many more. Authoritative captions provide statistics, background on each ship. 190 black-and-white photographs and illustrations. Introduction. 128pp. 8⅞ × 11¾. 27163-3 Pa. $12.95

CATALOG OF DOVER BOOKS

EARLY NINETEENTH-CENTURY CRAFTS AND TRADES, Peter Stockham (ed.). Extremely rare 1807 volume describes to youngsters the crafts and trades of the day: brickmaker, weaver, dressmaker, bookbinder, ropemaker, saddler, many more. Quaint prose, charming illustrations for each craft. 20 black-and-white line illustrations. 192pp. 4⅝ × 6. 27293-1 Pa. $4.95

VICTORIAN FASHIONS AND COSTUMES FROM HARPER'S BAZAR, 1867–1898, Stella Blum (ed.). Day costumes, evening wear, sports clothes, shoes, hats, other accessories in over 1,000 detailed engravings. 320pp. 9⅜ × 12¼.
22990-4 Pa. $13.95

GUSTAV STICKLEY, THE CRAFTSMAN, Mary Ann Smith. Superb study surveys broad scope of Stickley's achievement, especially in architecture. Design philosophy, rise and fall of the Craftsman empire, descriptions and floor plans for many Craftsman houses, more. 86 black-and-white halftones. 31 line illustrations. Introduction. 208pp. 6½ × 9¼. 27210-9 Pa. $9.95

THE LONG ISLAND RAIL ROAD IN EARLY PHOTOGRAPHS, Ron Ziel. Over 220 rare photos, informative text document origin (1844) and development of rail service on Long Island. Vintage views of early trains, locomotives, stations, passengers, crews, much more. Captions. 8⅞ × 11¾. 26301-0 Pa. $13.95

THE BOOK OF OLD SHIPS: From Egyptian Galleys to Clipper Ships, Henry B. Culver. Superb, authoritative history of sailing vessels, with 80 magnificent line illustrations. Galley, bark, caravel, longship, whaler, many more. Detailed, informative text on each vessel by noted naval historian. Introduction. 256pp. 5⅜ × 8½. 27332-6 Pa. $6.95

TEN BOOKS ON ARCHITECTURE, Vitruvius. The most important book ever written on architecture. Early Roman aesthetics, technology, classical orders, site selection, all other aspects. Morgan translation. 331pp. 5⅜ × 8½. 20645-9 Pa. $8.95

THE HUMAN FIGURE IN MOTION, Eadweard Muybridge. More than 4,500 stopped-action photos, in action series, showing undraped men, women, children jumping, lying down, throwing, sitting, wrestling, carrying, etc. 390pp. 7⅞ × 10⅝.
20204-6 Clothbd. $24.95

TREES OF THE EASTERN AND CENTRAL UNITED STATES AND CANADA, William M. Harlow. Best one-volume guide to 140 trees. Full descriptions, woodlore, range, etc. Over 600 illustrations. Handy size. 288pp. 4½ × 6⅜.
20395-6 Pa. $5.95

SONGS OF WESTERN BIRDS, Dr. Donald J. Borror. Complete song and call repertoire of 60 western species, including flycatchers, juncoes, cactus wrens, many more—includes fully illustrated booklet. Cassette and manual 99913-0 $8.95

GROWING AND USING HERBS AND SPICES, Milo Miloradovich. Versatile handbook provides all the information needed for cultivation and use of all the herbs and spices available in North America. 4 illustrations. Index. Glossary. 236pp. 5⅜ × 8½. 25058-X Pa. $5.95

BIG BOOK OF MAZES AND LABYRINTHS, Walter Shepherd. 50 mazes and labyrinths in all—classical, solid, ripple, and more—in one great volume. Perfect inexpensive puzzler for clever youngsters. Full solutions. 112pp. 8⅛ × 11.
22951-3 Pa. $3.95

PIANO TUNING, J. Cree Fischer. Clearest, best book for beginner, amateur. Simple repairs, raising dropped notes, tuning by easy method of flattened fifths. No previous skills needed. 4 illustrations. 201pp. 5⅜ × 8½. 23267-0 Pa. $5.95

A SOURCE BOOK IN THEATRICAL HISTORY, A. M. Nagler. Contemporary observers on acting, directing, make-up, costuming, stage props, machinery, scene design, from Ancient Greece to Chekhov. 611pp. 5⅜ × 8½. 20515-0 Pa. $11.95

THE COMPLETE NONSENSE OF EDWARD LEAR, Edward Lear. All nonsense limericks, zany alphabets, Owl and Pussycat, songs, nonsense botany, etc., illustrated by Lear. Total of 320pp. 5⅜ × 8½. (USO) 20167-8 Pa. $5.95

VICTORIAN PARLOUR POETRY: An Annotated Anthology, Michael R. Turner. 117 gems by Longfellow, Tennyson, Browning, many lesser-known poets. "The Village Blacksmith," "Curfew Must Not Ring Tonight," "Only a Baby Small," dozens more, often difficult to find elsewhere. Index of poets, titles, first lines. xxiii + 325pp. 5⅜ × 8¼. 27044-0 Pa. $8.95

DUBLINERS, James Joyce. Fifteen stories offer vivid, tightly focused observations of the lives of Dublin's poorer classes. At least one, "The Dead," is considered a masterpiece. Reprinted complete and unabridged from standard edition. 160pp. 5³⁄₁₆ × 8¼. 26870-5 Pa. $1.00

THE HAUNTED MONASTERY and THE CHINESE MAZE MURDERS, Robert van Gulik. Two full novels by van Gulik, set in 7th-century China, continue adventures of Judge Dee and his companions. An evil Taoist monastery, seemingly supernatural events; overgrown topiary maze hides strange crimes. 27 illustrations. 328pp. 5⅜ × 8½. 23502-5 Pa. $7.95

THE BOOK OF THE SACRED MAGIC OF ABRAMELIN THE MAGE, translated by S. MacGregor Mathers. Medieval manuscript of ceremonial magic. Basic document in Aleister Crowley, Golden Dawn groups. 268pp. 5⅜ × 8½. 23211-5 Pa. $7.95

NEW RUSSIAN-ENGLISH AND ENGLISH-RUSSIAN DICTIONARY, M. A. O'Brien. This is a remarkably handy Russian dictionary, containing a surprising amount of information, including over 70,000 entries. 366pp. 4½ × 6⅛. 20208-9 Pa. $8.95

HISTORIC HOMES OF THE AMERICAN PRESIDENTS, Second, Revised Edition, Irvin Haas. A traveler's guide to American Presidential homes, most open to the public, depicting and describing homes occupied by every American President from George Washington to George Bush. With visiting hours, admission charges, travel routes. 175 photographs. Index. 160pp. 8¼ × 11. 26751-2 Pa. $10.95

NEW YORK IN THE FORTIES, Andreas Feininger. 162 brilliant photographs by the well-known photographer, formerly with *Life* magazine. Commuters, shoppers, Times Square at night, much else from city at its peak. Captions by John von Hartz. 181pp. 9¼ × 10¾. 23585-8 Pa. $12.95

INDIAN SIGN LANGUAGE, William Tomkins. Over 525 signs developed by Sioux and other tribes. Written instructions and diagrams. Also 290 pictographs. 111pp. 6⅛ × 9¼. 22029-X Pa. $3.50

CATALOG OF DOVER BOOKS

ANATOMY: A Complete Guide for Artists, Joseph Sheppard. A master of figure drawing shows artists how to render human anatomy convincingly. Over 460 illustrations. 224pp. 8⅜ × 11¼. 27279-6 Pa. $9.95

MEDIEVAL CALLIGRAPHY: Its History and Technique, Marc Drogin. Spirited history, comprehensive instruction manual covers 13 styles (ca. 4th century thru 15th). Excellent photographs; directions for duplicating medieval techniques with modern tools. 224pp. 8⅜ × 11¼. 26142-5 Pa. $11.95

DRIED FLOWERS: How to Prepare Them, Sarah Whitlock and Martha Rankin. Complete instructions on how to use silica gel, meal and borax, perlite aggregate, sand and borax, glycerine and water to create attractive permanent flower arrangements. 12 illustrations. 32pp. 5⅜ × 8½. 21802-3 Pa. $1.00

EASY-TO-MAKE BIRD FEEDERS FOR WOODWORKERS, Scott D. Campbell. Detailed, simple-to-use guide for designing, constructing, caring for and using feeders. Text, illustrations for 12 classic and contemporary designs. 96pp. 5⅜ × 8½. 25847-5 Pa. $2.95

OLD-TIME CRAFTS AND TRADES, Peter Stockham. An 1807 book created to teach children about crafts and trades open to them as future careers. It describes in detailed, nontechnical terms 24 different occupations, among them coachmaker, gardener, hairdresser, lacemaker, shoemaker, wheelwright, copper-plate printer, milliner, trunkmaker, merchant and brewer. Finely detailed engravings illustrate each occupation. 192pp. 4⅝ × 6. 27398-9 Pa. $4.95

THE HISTORY OF UNDERCLOTHES, C. Willett Cunnington and Phyllis Cunnington. Fascinating, well-documented survey covering six centuries of English undergarments, enhanced with over 100 illustrations: 12th-century laced-up bodice, footed long drawers (1795), 19th-century bustles, 19th-century corsets for men, Victorian "bust improvers," much more. 272pp. 5⅝ × 8¼. 27124-2 Pa. $9.95

ARTS AND CRAFTS FURNITURE: The Complete Brooks Catalog of 1912, Brooks Manufacturing Co. Photos and detailed descriptions of more than 150 now very collectible furniture designs from the Arts and Crafts movement depict davenports, settees, buffets, desks, tables, chairs, bedsteads, dressers and more, all built of solid, quarter-sawed oak. Invaluable for students and enthusiasts of antiques, Americana and the decorative arts. 80pp. 6½ × 9¼. 27471-3 Pa. $7.95

HOW WE INVENTED THE AIRPLANE: An Illustrated History, Orville Wright. Fascinating firsthand account covers early experiments, construction of planes and motors, first flights, much more. Introduction and commentary by Fred C. Kelly. 76 photographs. 96pp. 8¼ × 11. 25662-6 Pa. $7.95

THE ARTS OF THE SAILOR: Knotting, Splicing and Ropework, Hervey Garrett Smith. Indispensable shipboard reference covers tools, basic knots and useful hitches; handsewing and canvas work, more. Over 100 illustrations. Delightful reading for sea lovers. 256pp. 5⅜ × 8½. 26440-8 Pa. $7.95

FRANK LLOYD WRIGHT'S FALLINGWATER: The House and Its History, Second, Revised Edition, Donald Hoffmann. A total revision—both in text and illustrations—of the standard document on Fallingwater, the boldest, most personal architectural statement of Wright's mature years, updated with valuable new material from the recently opened Frank Lloyd Wright Archives. "Fascinating"—*The New York Times*. 116 illustrations. 128pp. 9¼ × 10¾. 27430-6 Pa. $10.95

PHOTOGRAPHIC SKETCHBOOK OF THE CIVIL WAR, Alexander Gardner. 100 photos taken on field during the Civil War. Famous shots of Manassas, Harper's Ferry, Lincoln, Richmond, slave pens, etc. 244pp. 10⅝ × 8¼.
22731-6 Pa. $9.95

FIVE ACRES AND INDEPENDENCE, Maurice G. Kains. Great back-to-the-land classic explains basics of self-sufficient farming. The one book to get. 95 illustrations. 397pp. 5⅜ × 8½.
20974-1 Pa. $6.95

SONGS OF EASTERN BIRDS, Dr. Donald J. Borror. Songs and calls of 60 species most common to eastern U.S.: warblers, woodpeckers, flycatchers, thrushes, larks, many more in high-quality recording.
Cassette and manual 99912-2 $8.95

A MODERN HERBAL, Margaret Grieve. Much the fullest, most exact, most useful compilation of herbal material. Gigantic alphabetical encyclopedia, from aconite to zedoary, gives botanical information, medical properties, folklore, economic uses, much else. Indispensable to serious reader. 161 illustrations. 888pp. 6½ × 9¼.
2-vol. set. (USO)
Vol. I: 22798-7 Pa. $9.95
Vol. II: 22799-5 Pa. $9.95

HIDDEN TREASURE MAZE BOOK, Dave Phillips. Solve 34 challenging mazes accompanied by heroic tales of adventure. Evil dragons, people-eating plants, bloodthirsty giants, many more dangerous adversaries lurk at every twist and turn. 34 mazes, stories, solutions. 48pp. 8¼ × 11.
24566-7 Pa. $2.95

LETTERS OF W. A. MOZART, Wolfgang A. Mozart. Remarkable letters show bawdy wit, humor, imagination, musical insights, contemporary musical world; includes some letters from Leopold Mozart. 276pp. 5⅜ × 8½.
22859-2 Pa. $6.95

BASIC PRINCIPLES OF CLASSICAL BALLET, Agrippina Vaganova. Great Russian theoretician, teacher explains methods for teaching classical ballet. 118 illustrations. 175pp. 5⅜ × 8½.
22036-2 Pa. $4.95

THE JUMPING FROG, Mark Twain. Revenge edition. The original story of The Celebrated Jumping Frog of Calaveras County, a hapless French translation, and Twain's hilarious "retranslation" from the French. 12 illustrations. 66pp. 5⅜ × 8½.
22686-7 Pa. $3.50

BEST REMEMBERED POEMS, Martin Gardner (ed.). The 126 poems in this superb collection of 19th- and 20th-century British and American verse range from Shelley's "To a Skylark" to the impassioned "Renascence" of Edna St. Vincent Millay and to Edward Lear's whimsical "The Owl and the Pussycat." 224pp. 5⅜ × 8½.
27165-X Pa. $4.95

COMPLETE SONNETS, William Shakespeare. Over 150 exquisite poems deal with love, friendship, the tyranny of time, beauty's evanescence, death and other themes in language of remarkable power, precision and beauty. Glossary of archaic terms. 80pp. 5³⁄₁₆ × 8¼.
26686-9 Pa. $1.00

BODIES IN A BOOKSHOP, R. T. Campbell. Challenging mystery of blackmail and murder with ingenious plot and superbly drawn characters. In the best tradition of British suspense fiction. 192pp. 5⅜ × 8½.
24720-1 Pa. $5.95

THE INFLUENCE OF SEA POWER UPON HISTORY, 1660–1783, A. T. Mahan. Influential classic of naval history and tactics still used as text in war colleges. First paperback edition. 4 maps. 24 battle plans. 640pp. 5⅜ × 8½.
25509-3 Pa. $12.95

THE STORY OF THE TITANIC AS TOLD BY ITS SURVIVORS, Jack Winocour (ed.). What it was really like. Panic, despair, shocking inefficiency, and a little heroism. More thrilling than any fictional account. 26 illustrations. 320pp. 5⅜ × 8½.
20610-6 Pa. $7.95

FAIRY AND FOLK TALES OF THE IRISH PEASANTRY, William Butler Yeats (ed.). Treasury of 64 tales from the twilight world of Celtic myth and legend: "The Soul Cages," "The Kildare Pooka," "King O'Toole and his Goose," many more. Introduction and Notes by W. B. Yeats. 352pp. 5⅜ × 8½.
26941-8 Pa. $7.95

BUDDHIST MAHAYANA TEXTS, E. B. Cowell and Others (eds.). Superb, accurate translations of basic documents in Mahayana Buddhism, highly important in history of religions. The Buddha-karita of Asvaghosha, Larger Sukhavativyuha, more. 448pp. 5⅜ × 8½. ,
25552-2 Pa. $9.95

ONE TWO THREE . . . INFINITY: Facts and Speculations of Science, George Gamow. Great physicist's fascinating, readable overview of contemporary science: number theory, relativity, fourth dimension, entropy, genes, atomic structure, much more. 128 illustrations. Index. 352pp. 5⅜ × 8½.
25664-2 Pa. $8.95

ENGINEERING IN HISTORY, Richard Shelton Kirby, et al. Broad, nontechnical survey of history's major technological advances: birth of Greek science, industrial revolution, electricity and applied science, 20th-century automation, much more. 181 illustrations. ". . . excellent . . ."—Isis. Bibliography. vii + 530pp. 5⅜ × 8¼.
26412-2 Pa. $14.95